t10.99

Easy Piano

D1789288

Classic

Children's Songs

Fun Songs to Play and Sing!

Arranged by Jan L. Harrison

Illustrated by Jon Kirby

Classic Children's Songs

Table of Contents

Git Along Little Dogies

2. Early in the springtime we'll round up the dogies,
Slap on their brands and bob off their tails;
Round up our horses, load up the chuck wagon,
Then throw those dogies upon the trail.

3. It's whooping and yelling and driving the dogies,
Oh, how I wish you would go on,
It's whooping and punching and go on, little dogies,
For you know Wyoming will be your new home.

4. Some of the boys goes up the trail for pleasure,
But that's where they git it most awfully wrong;
For you haven't any idea the trouble they give us,
When we go driving them dogies along.

5. When the night comes on and we hold them
On the bed-ground,
These little dogies that roll on so slow;
Roll up the herd and cut out the strays,
And roll the little dogies that never rolled before.

6. Your mother she was raised way down in Texas,
Where the jimson weed and sandburs grow;
Now we'll fill you up on prickly pear and cholla,
Till you are ready for the trail to Idaho.

Blue Tail Fly
(Jimmy Crack Corn)

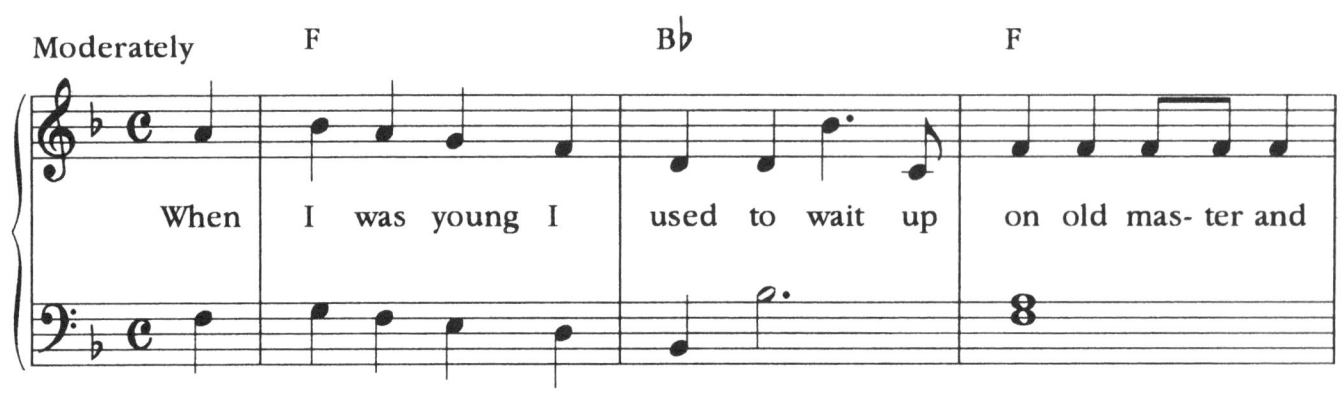

When I was young I used to wait up on old mas- ter and

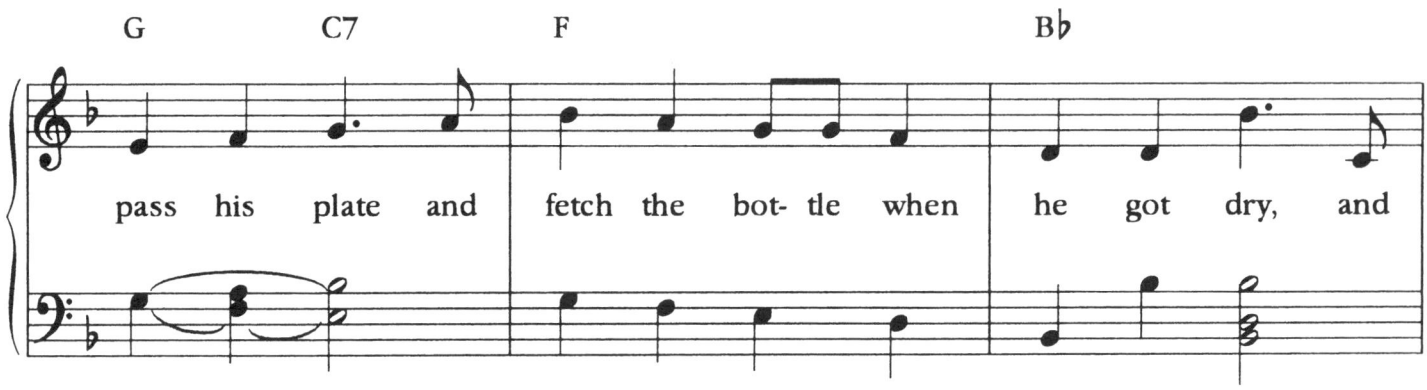

pass his plate and fetch the bot- tle when he got dry, and

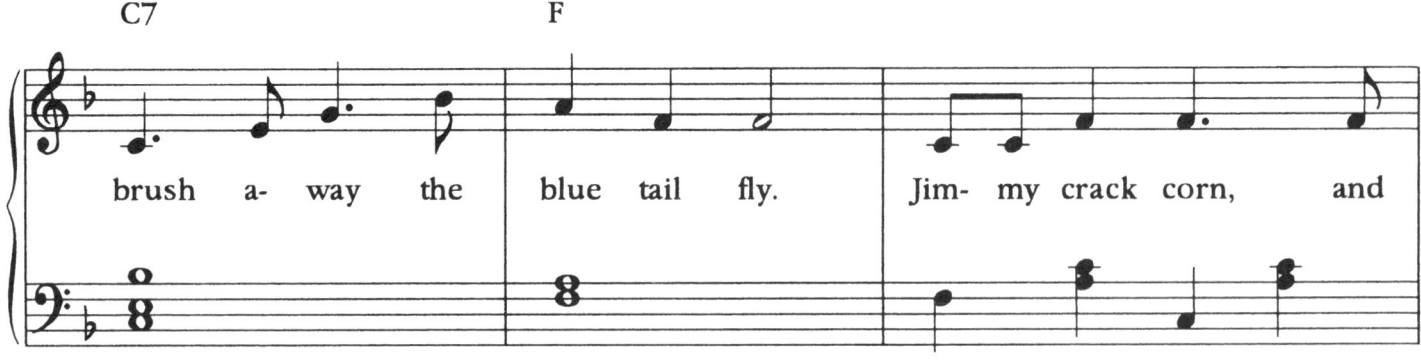

brush a- way the blue tail fly. Jim- my crack corn, and

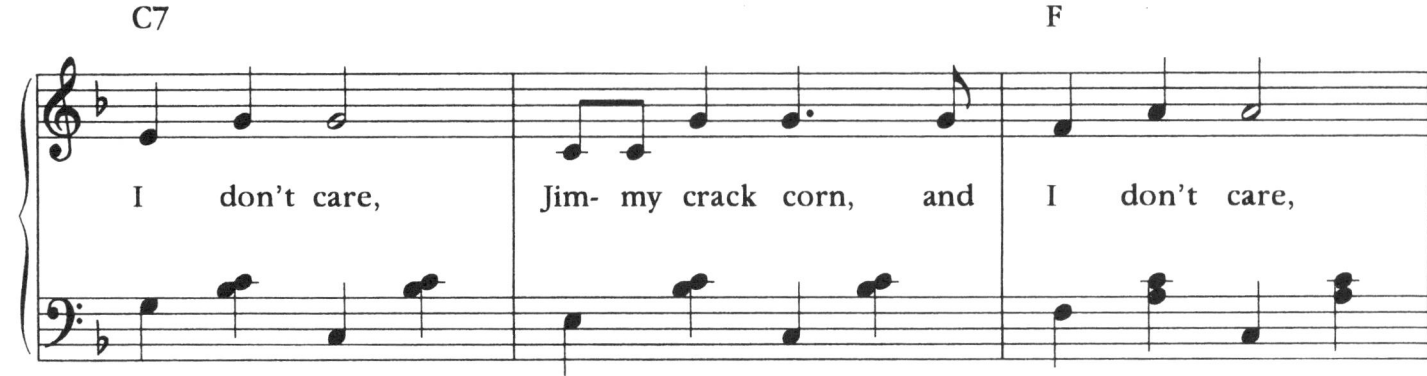

I don't care, Jim- my crack corn, and I don't care,

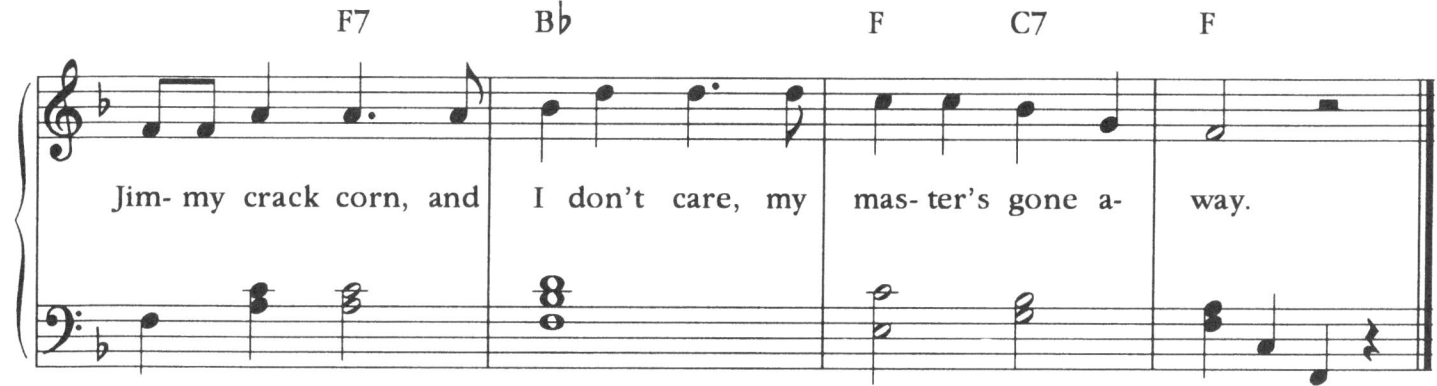

Jim- my crack corn, and | I don't care, my | mas- ter's gone a- | way.

2. And when he'd ride in the afternoon,
   I'd follow with a hickory broom;
   The pony being very shy,
   Got bitten by a blue-tail fly.
   Chorus:

3. One day he rode around the farm,
   The flies so numerous, they did swarm,
   One chanced to bite him on the thigh,
   The devil take the blue-tail fly.
   Chorus:

4. The pony run, he jump, he pitch,
   He threw old Master in a ditch;
   He died and the jury wondered why
   The verdict was the blue-tail fly.
   Chorus:

5. They laid him under a 'simmon tree,
   His epitaph is there to see;
   "Beneath the earth I'm forced to lie,
   A victim of the blue-tail fly."
   Chorus:

Alternate Verses

2. We went riding one afternoon,
   I followed with a hickory broom,
   The pony being very shy,
   Got bitten by a blue-tail fly.
   Chorus:

3. The pony he did rear and pitch,
   He threw old Master in a ditch;
   The jury asked the reason why,
   The verdict was the blue-tail fly.
   Chorus:

4. So we laid old Master down to rest;
   And on a stone this last request;
   "Beneath the earth I'm forced to lie,
   A victim of the blue-tail fly."
   Chorus:

Cock-A-Doodle-Doo

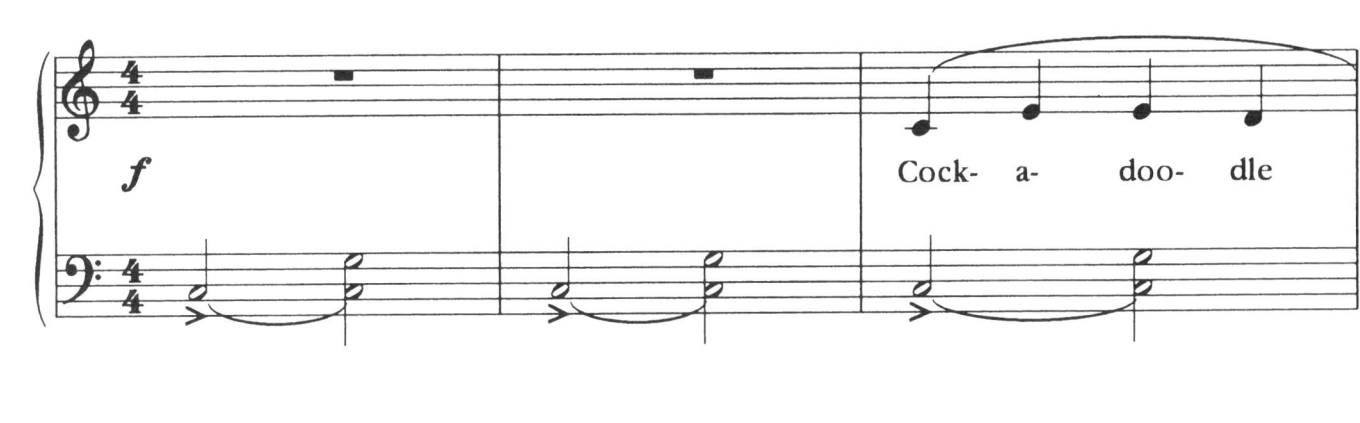

f

Cock- a- doo- dle

doo! My dame has lost her shoe. My

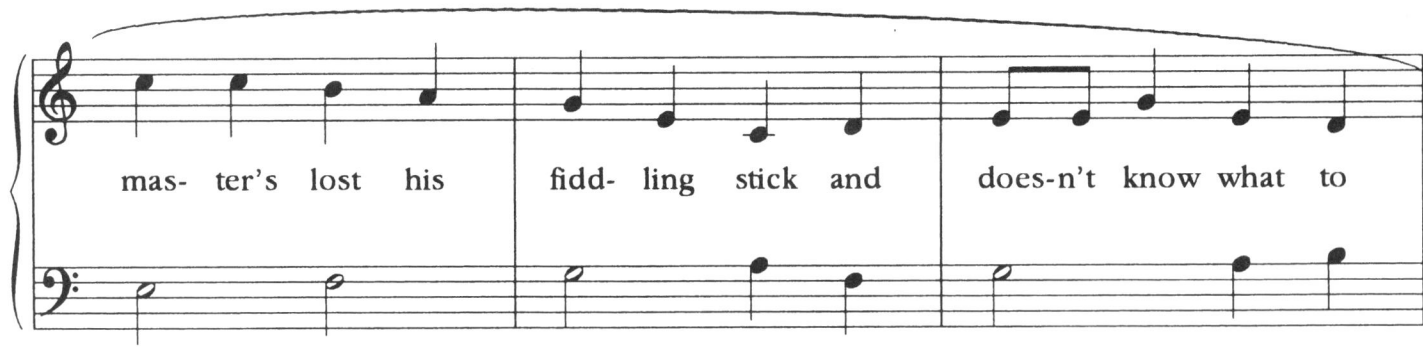

mas- ter's lost his fidd- ling stick and does-n't know what to

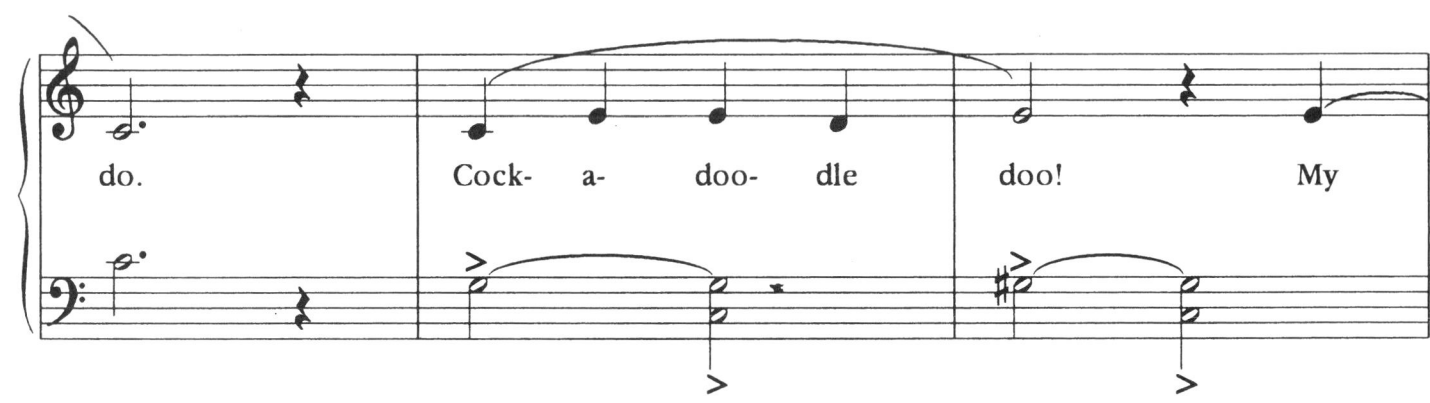

do. Cock- a- doo- dle doo! My

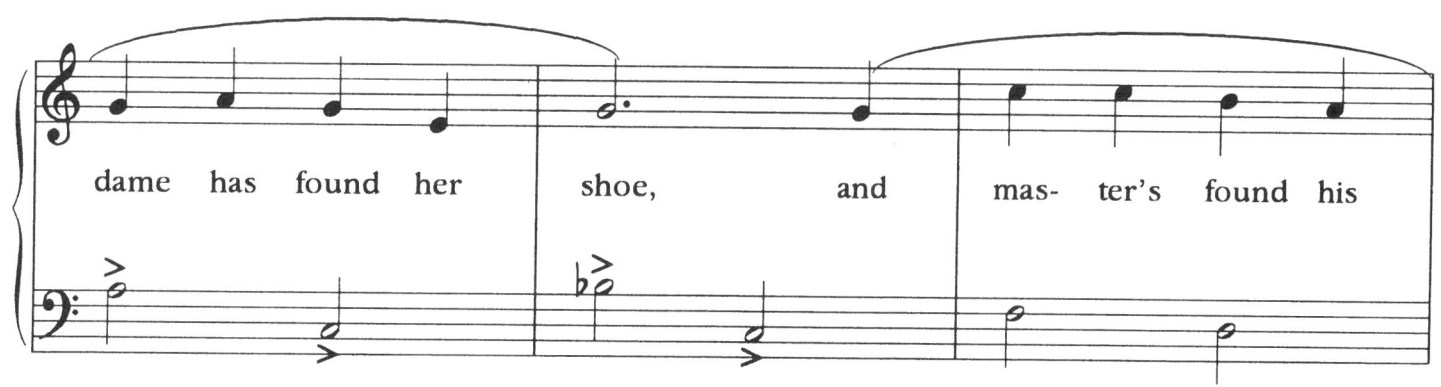

dame has found her shoe, and mas- ter's found his

fidd- ling stick, sing doo- dle doo- dle doo.

Georgie Porgie

Billy Groggin's Goat (Echo Song)

Traditional

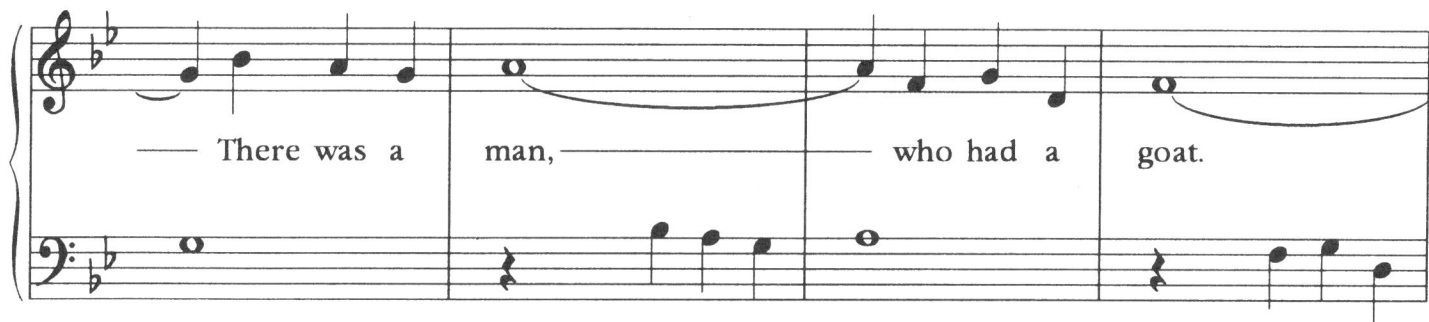

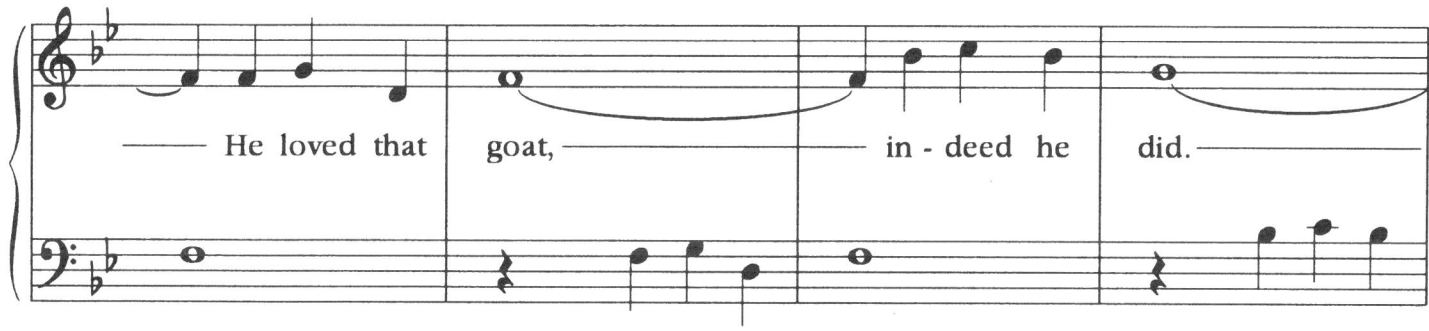

2. One day that goat felt frisk and fine;
   Ate three red shirts right off the line.
   The man, he grabbed him by the back,
   And tied him to a railroad track.

3. Now, when that train hove into sight,
   That goat grew pale and green with fright.
   He heaved a sigh, as if in pain;
   Coughed up the shirts and flagged the train.

She'll Be Comin' 'Round The Mountain

Traditional

Brightly

She'll be com-in' 'round the moun-tain when she comes.

She'll be com-'in 'round the moun-tain when she

comes. She'll be com- in' 'round the

moun- tain, she'll be com- in' 'round the moun- tain, she'll be

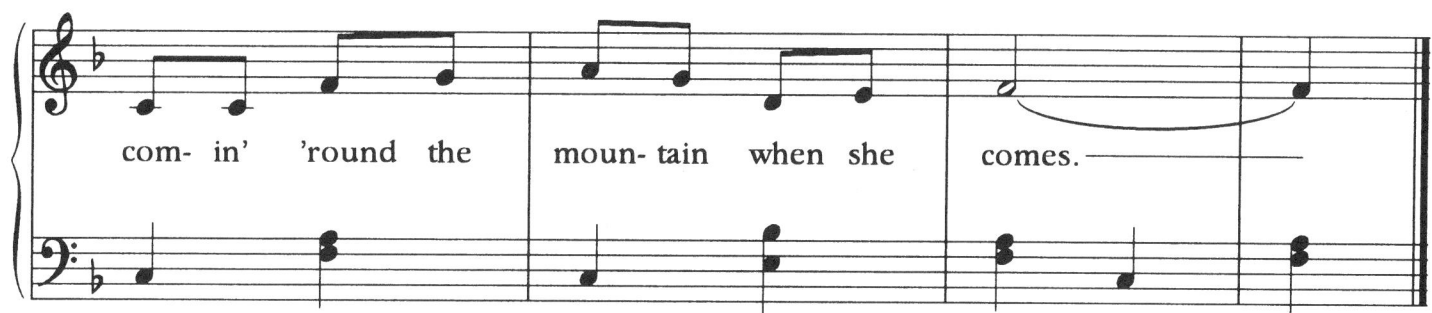

com- in' 'round the moun- tain when she comes.

2. She'll be drivin' six white horses when she comes, etc.

3. Oh, we'll all go out to meet her when she comes, etc.

4. We'll be singin' "hallelujah" when she comes, etc.

5. We will kill the old red rooster when she comes, etc.

6. And we'll all have chick'n and dumplin's when she comes, etc.

If You're Happy And You Know It

Traditional

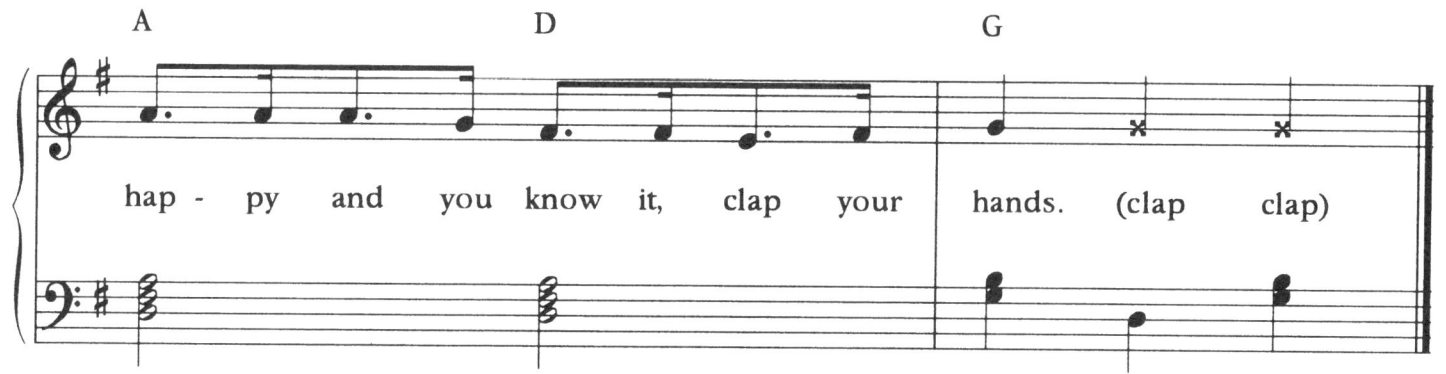

A
D
G
hap - py and you know it, clap your
hands. (clap clap)

2. If you're happy and you know it, tap your toe; (tap, tap)
If you're happy and you know it, tap your toe; (tap, tap)
If you're happy and you know it, etc.

3. If you're happy and you know it, nod your head; (nod, nod)
If you're happy and you know it, nod your head; (nod, nod)
If you're happy and you know it, etc.

Tom, Tom, The Piper's Son

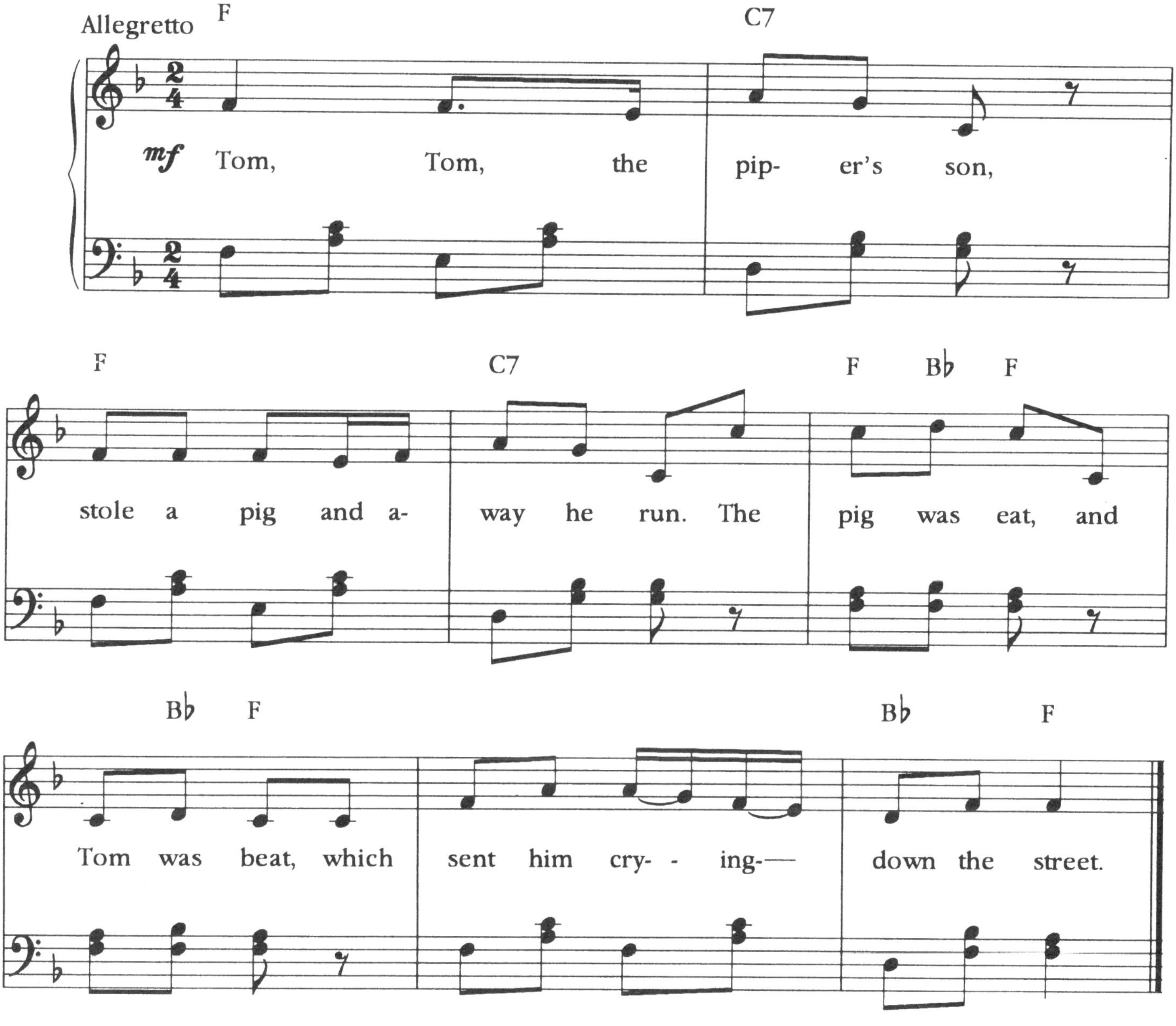
Allegretto
F
C7
mf
Tom, Tom, the pip- er's son,
F
C7
F Bb F
stole a pig and a- way he run. The pig was eat, and
Bb F
Bb F
Tom was beat, which sent him cry- - ing— down the street.

Home Sweet Home

Henry Bishop

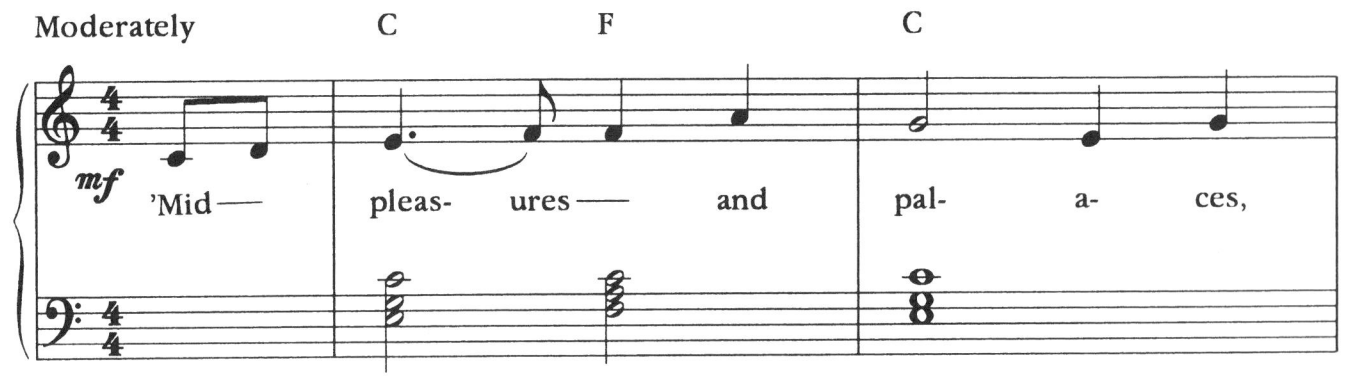

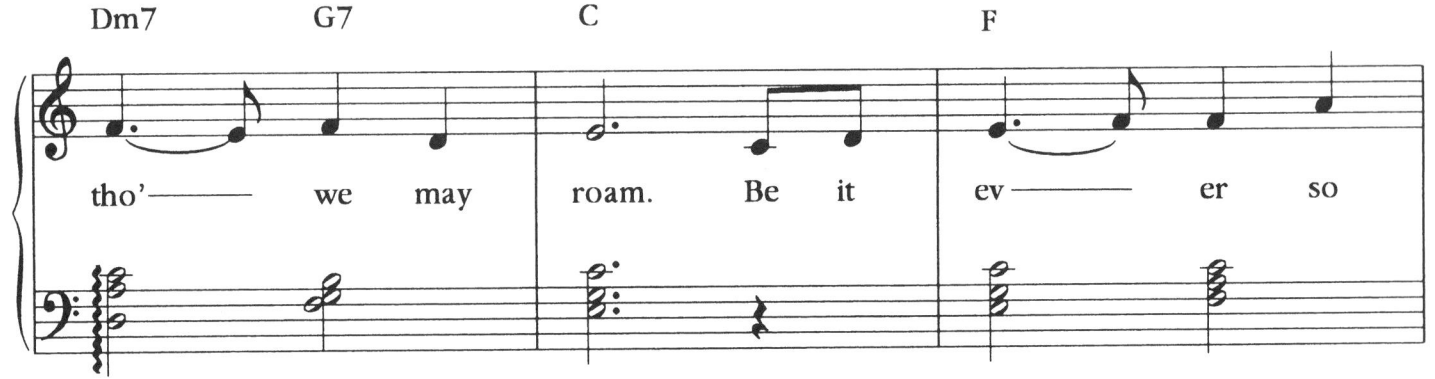

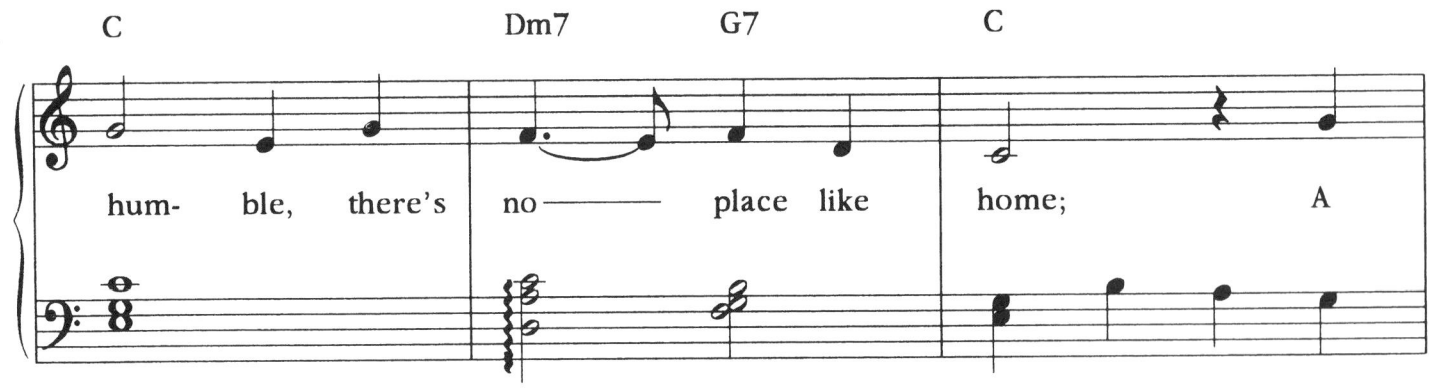

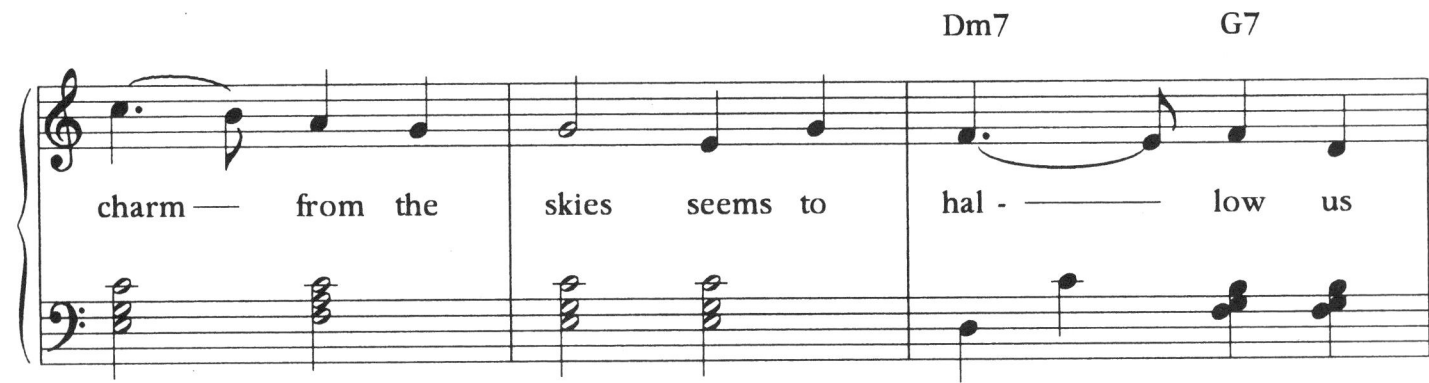

2. An exile from home, splendor dazzles in vain,
Oh, give me my lowly thatched cottage again;
The birds singing gaily, that come at my call;
Give me them, with that peace of mind, dearer
Than all.

3. To thee, I'll return, overburdened with care,
The heart's dearest solace will smile on me there.
No more from that cottage again will I roam,
Be it ever so humble, there's no place like home.

Eency Weency Spider

Traditional

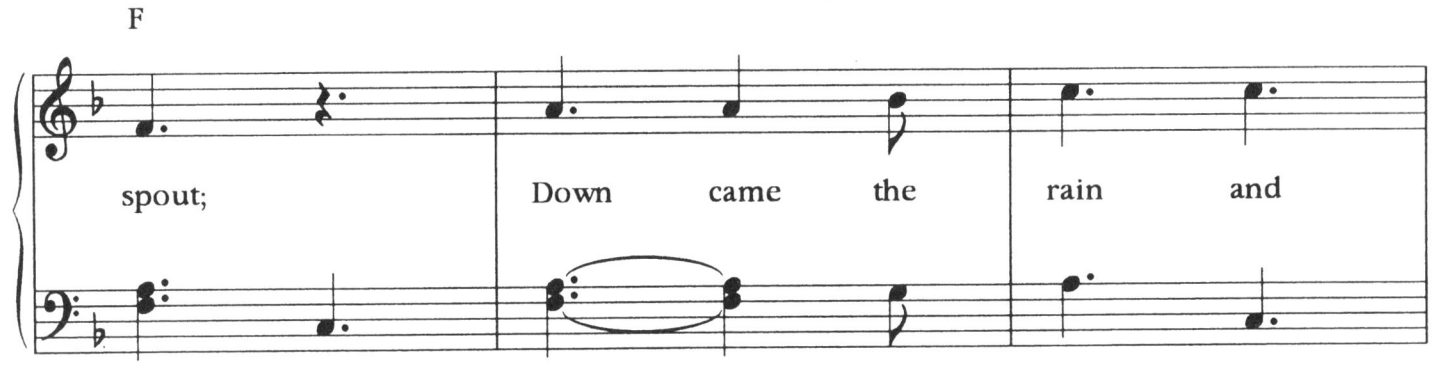

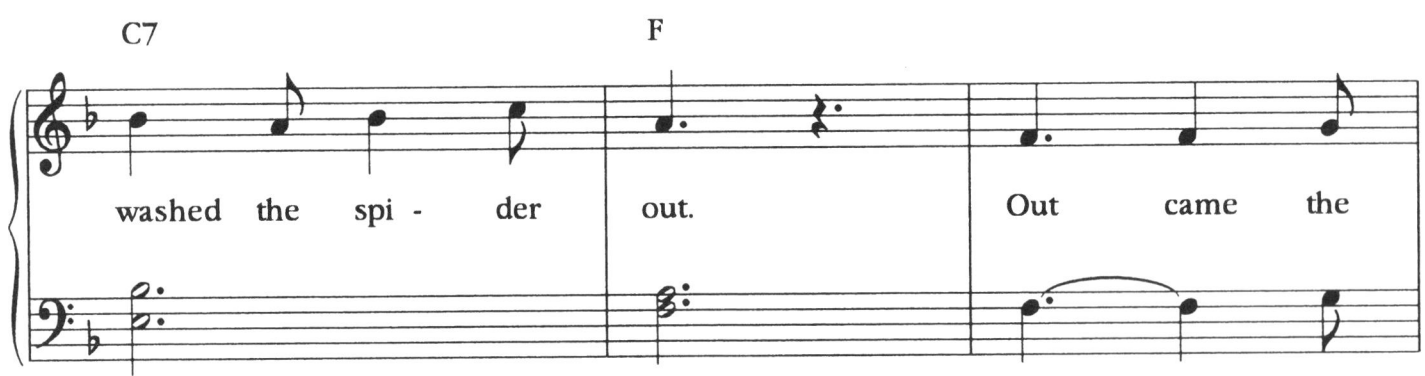

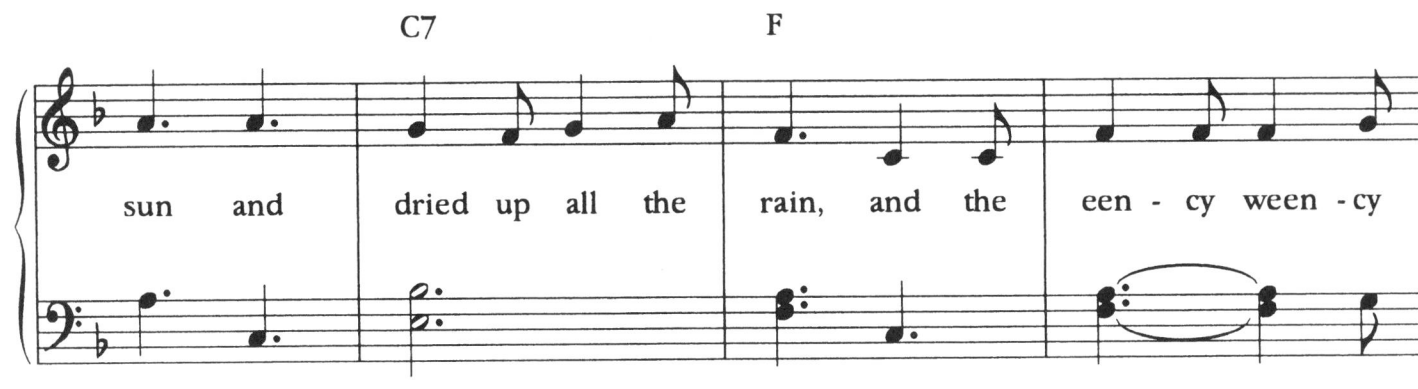

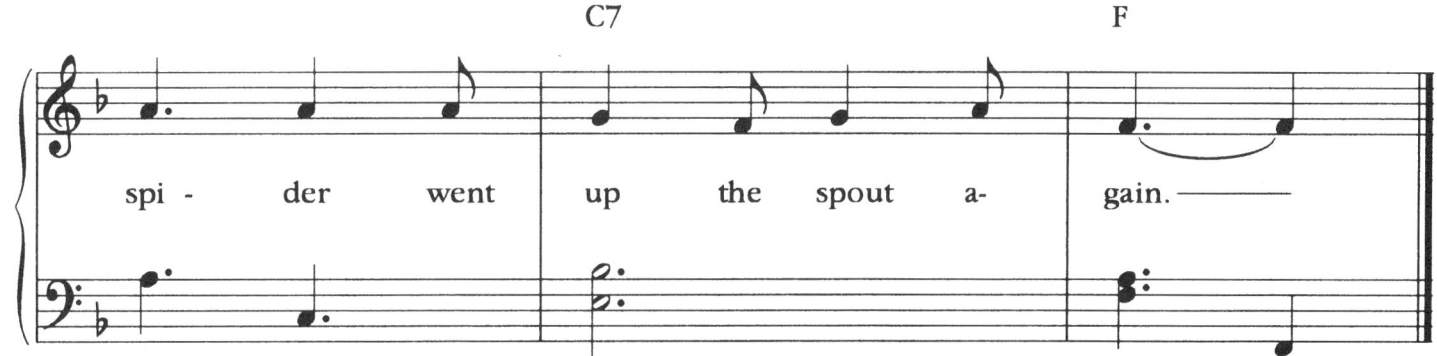

spi - der went | up the spout a- | gain.

Hey Diddle Diddle

Mother Goose

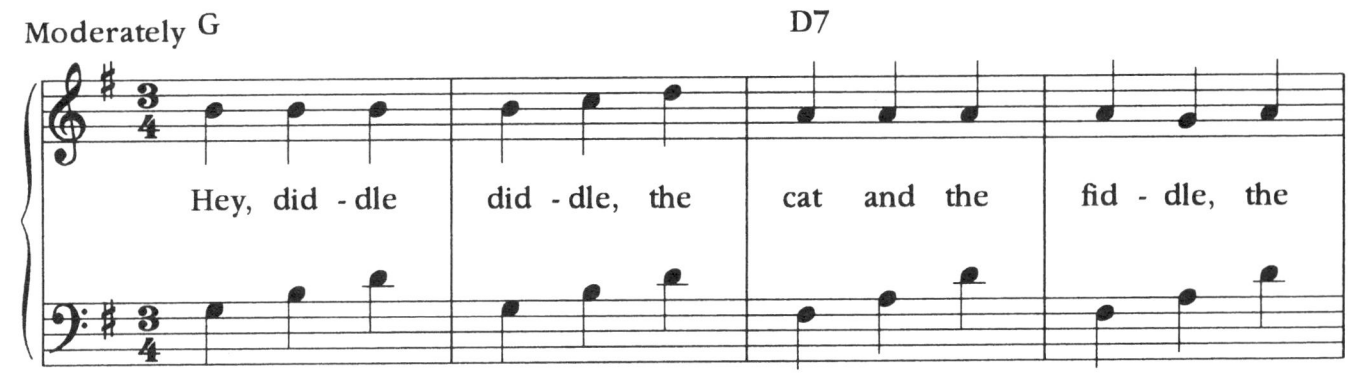

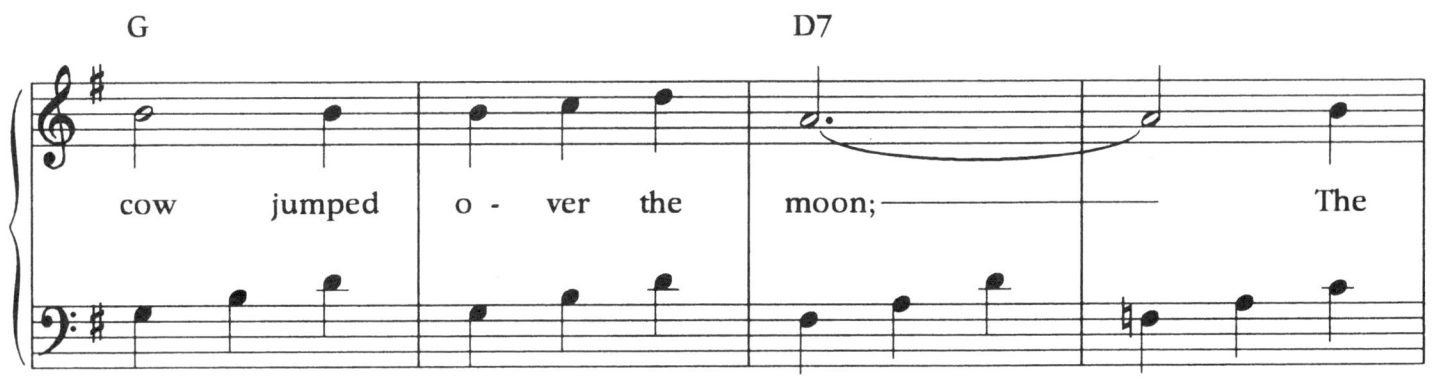

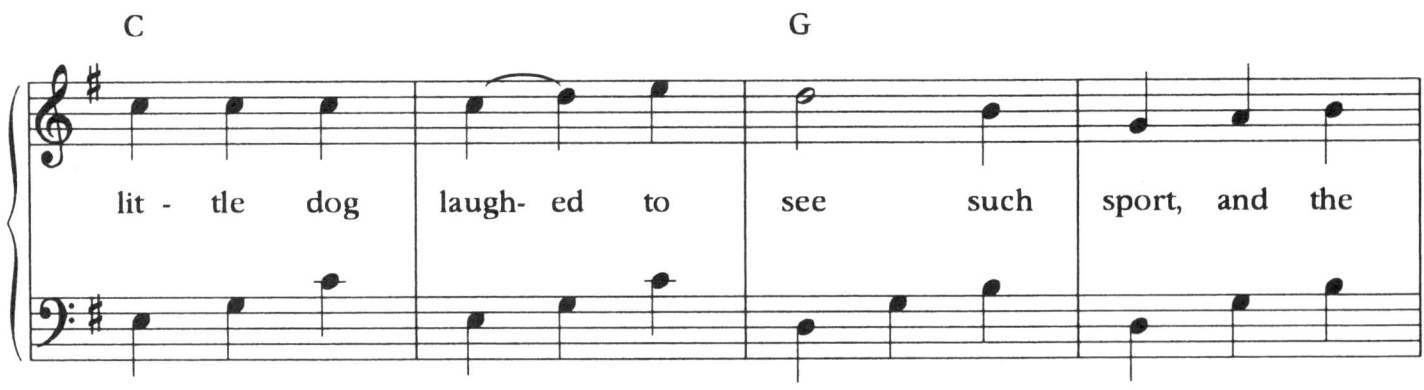

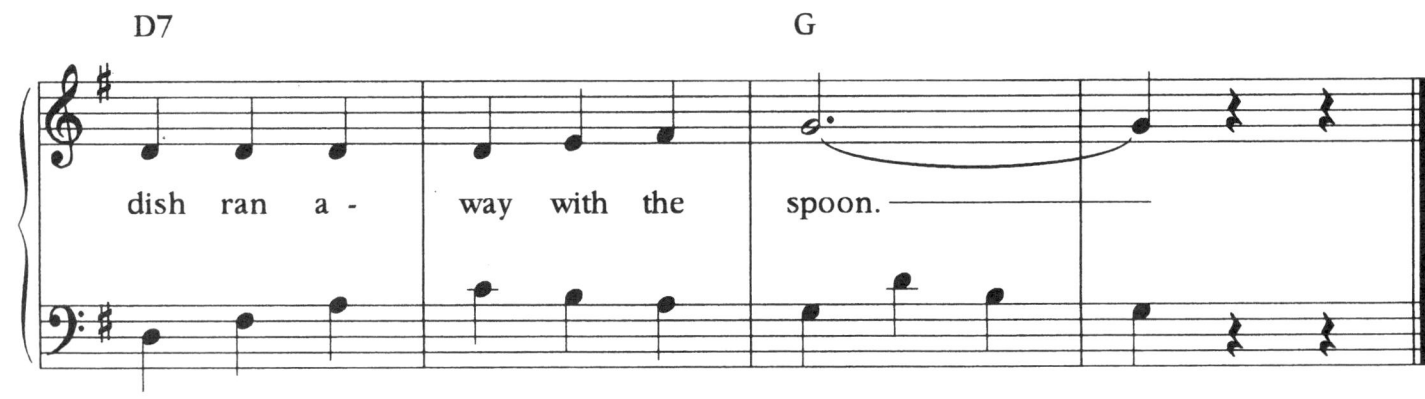

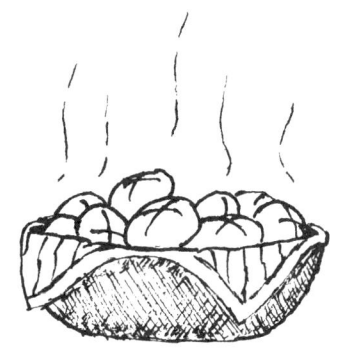

Hot Cross Buns

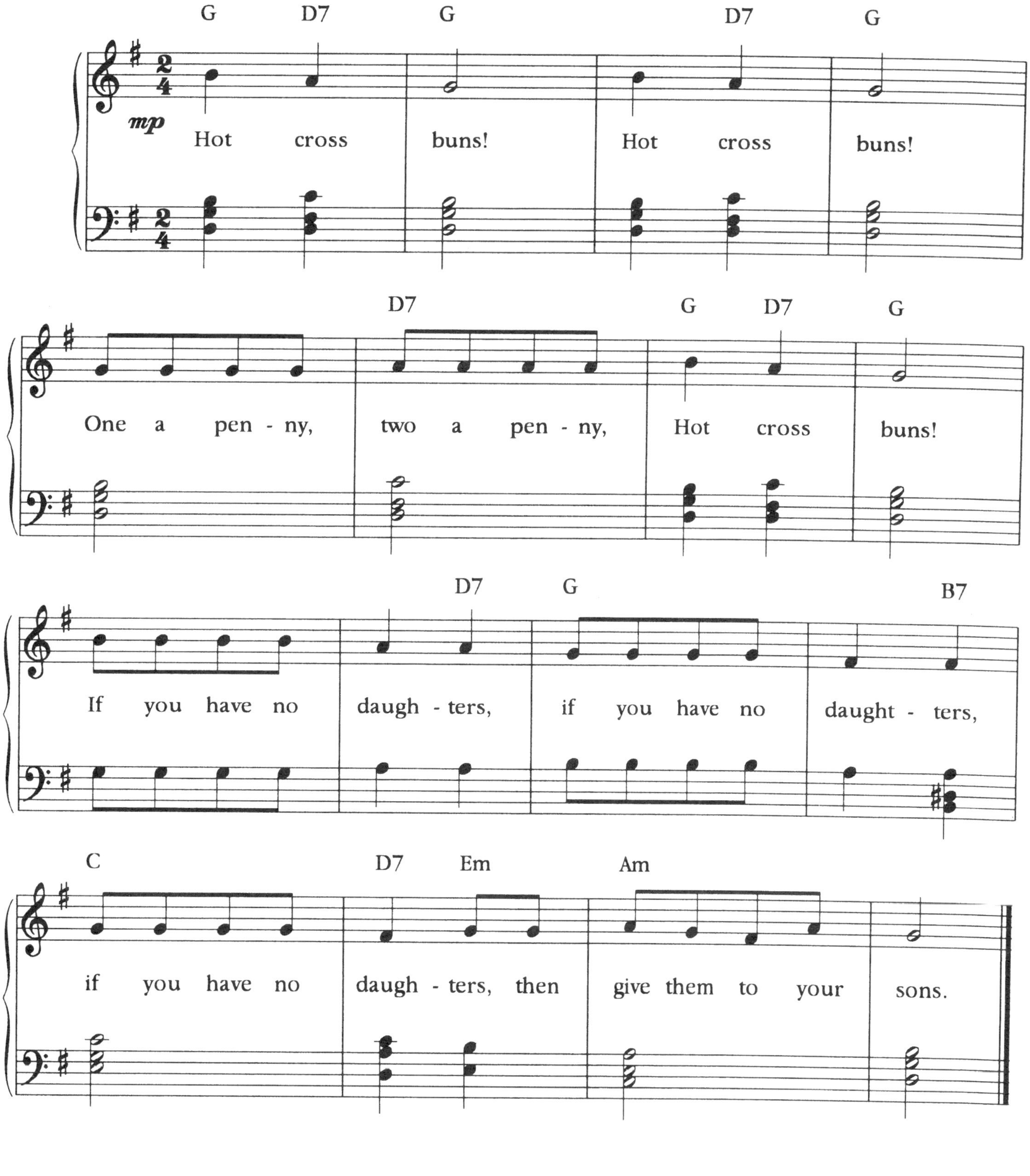
G D7 G D7 G
mp
Hot cross buns! Hot cross buns!
D7 G D7 G
One a pen - ny, two a pen - ny, Hot cross buns!
D7 G B7
If you have no daugh - ters, if you have no daught - ters,
C D7 Em Am
if you have no daugh - ters, then give them to your sons.

Over The River

Traditional

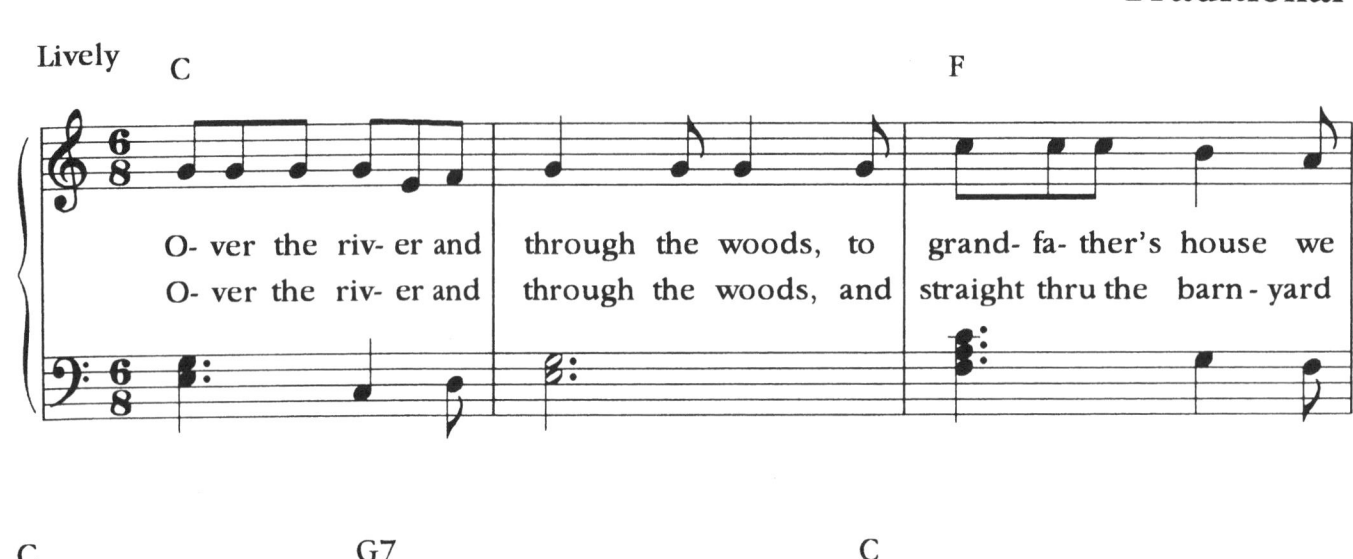

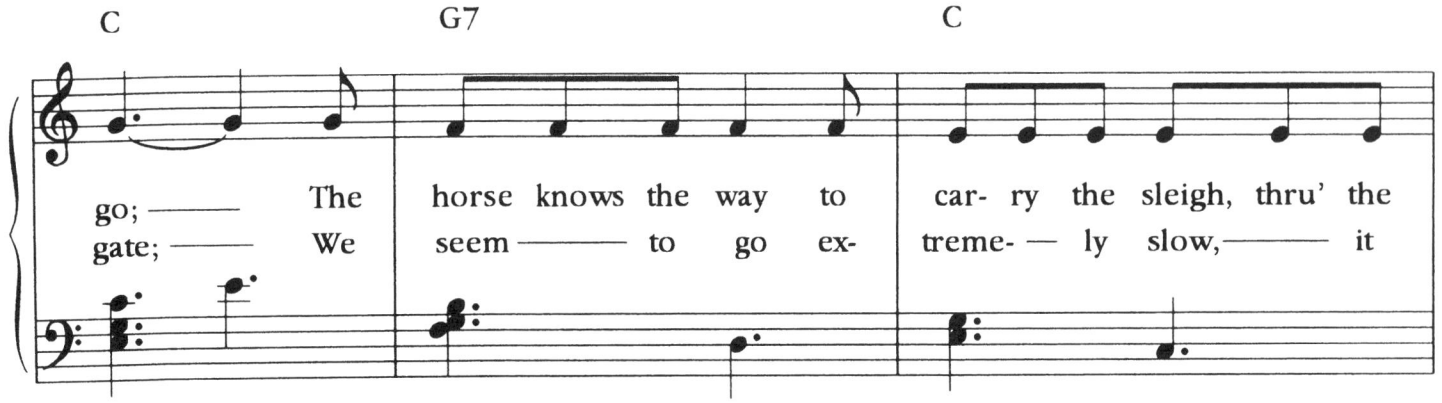

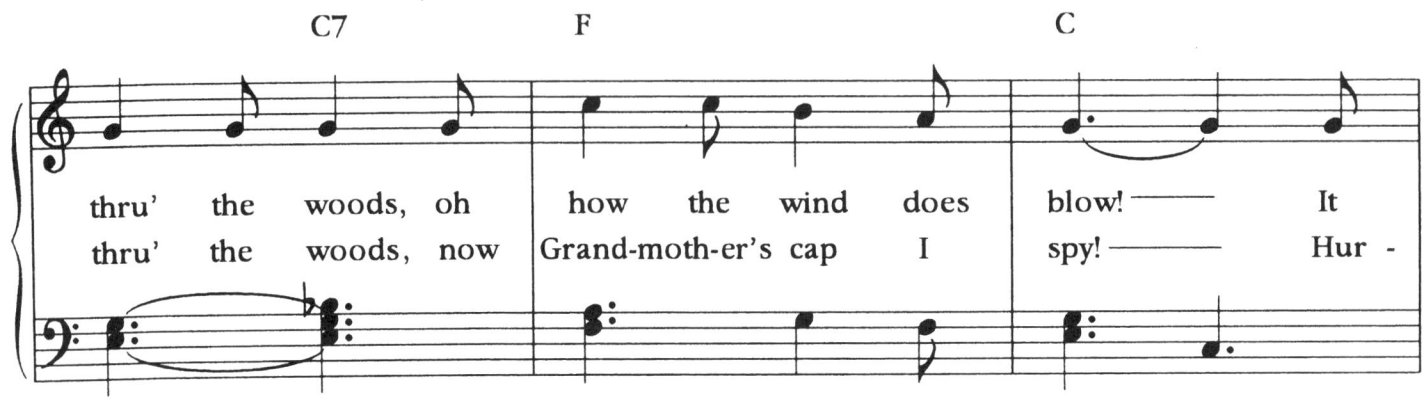

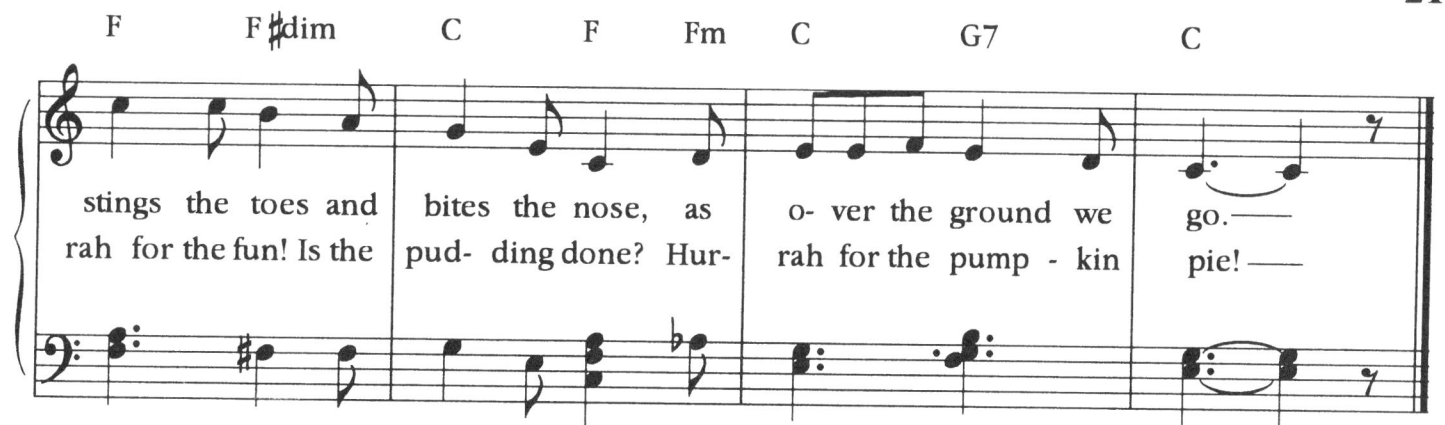

stings the toes and | bites the nose, as | o- ver the ground we | go.——

rah for the fun! Is the | pud- ding done? Hur- | rah for the pump - kin | pie! ——

Peter, Peter Pumpkin Eater

Moderately

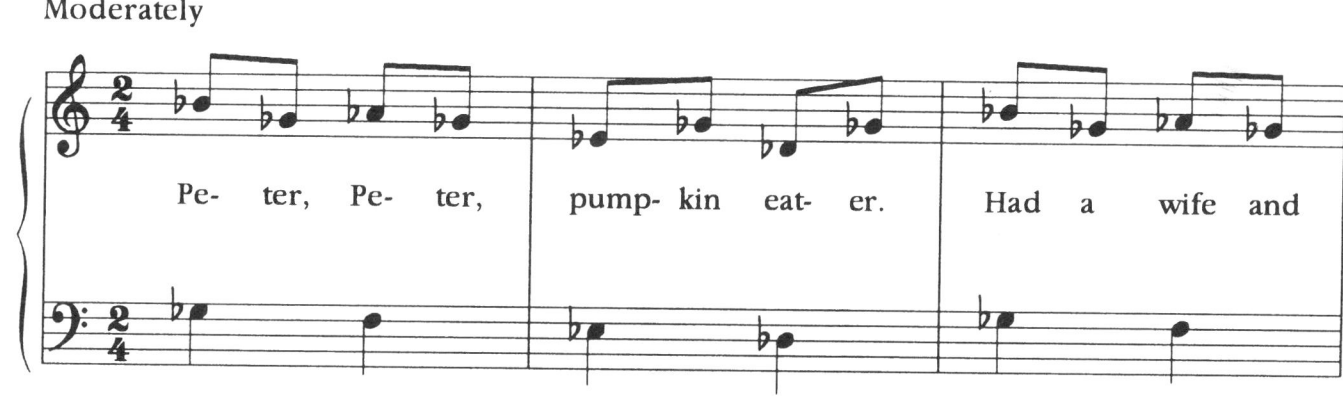

Pe- ter, Pe- ter, | pump- kin eat- er. | Had a wife and

could- n't keep her, | put her in a

pump- kin shell, and | there he kept her | ver- y well.

Humpty Dumpty

Mother Goose

C   G7   C

Hump- ty   Dump- ty   sat   on   a   wall,   Hump- ty   Dump- ty

G7   C   F   C

had   a   great   fall;   All   the   king's   hors- es   and

G7   A7   Dm   C   G7   C

all   the   king's   men   could- n't   put   Hump- ty   to-   geth- er   a - gain.

Hush Little Baby

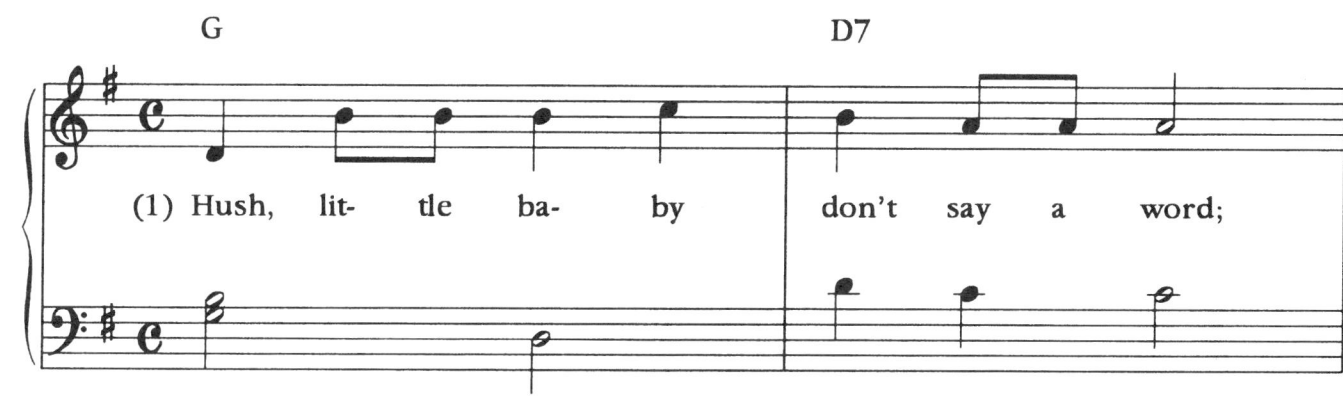

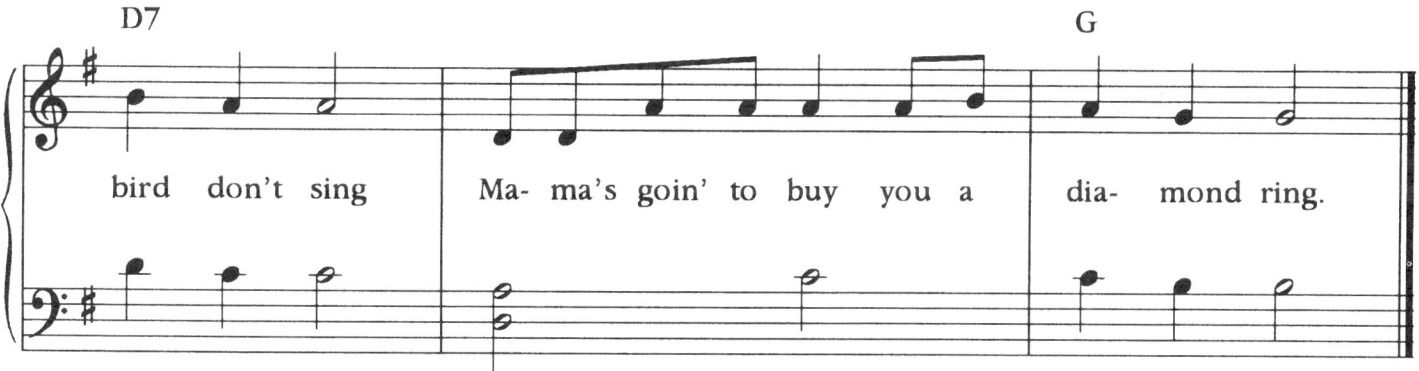

3. If that diamond ring turns brass

   Mama's goin' to buy you a looking glass.

4. If that looking glass gets broke,

   Mama's goin' to buy you a billy goat.

5. If that billy goat won't pull,

   Mama's goin' to buy you a cart and bull.

6. If that cart and bull turn over,

   Mama's goin' to buy you a dog named Rover.

7. If that dog named Rover won't bark,

   Mama's goin' to buy you a horse and cart.

8. If that horse and cart fall down,

   You'll still be the sweetest little baby in town.

Old MacDonald Had A Farm

Traditional

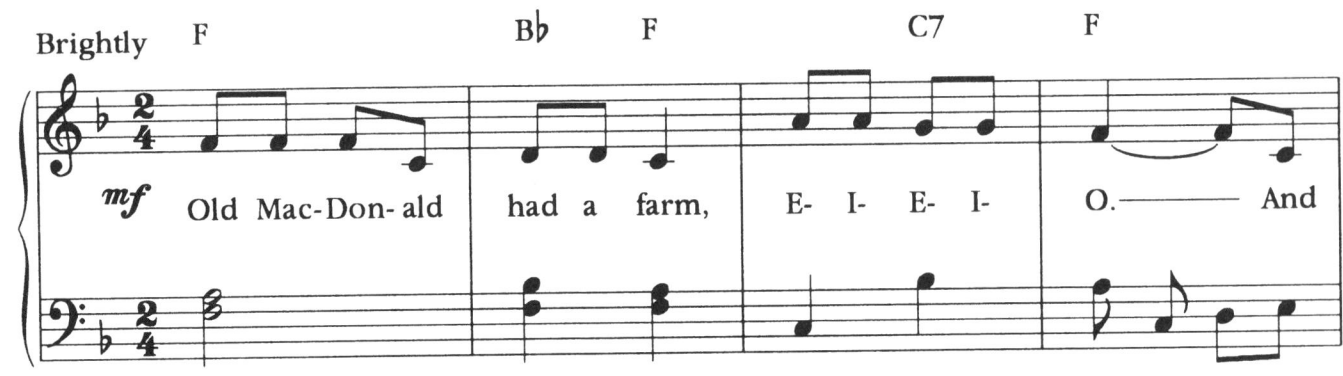

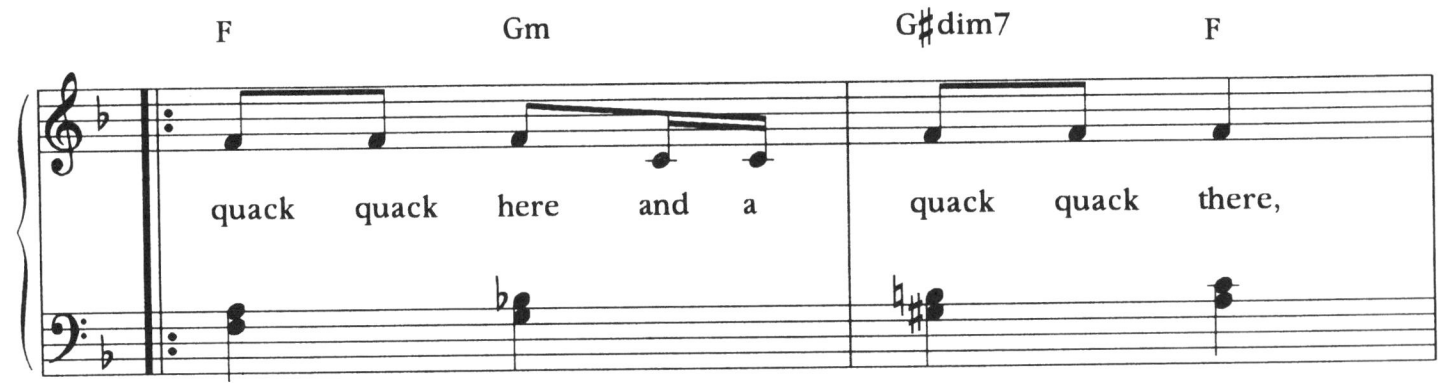

Repeat as necessary

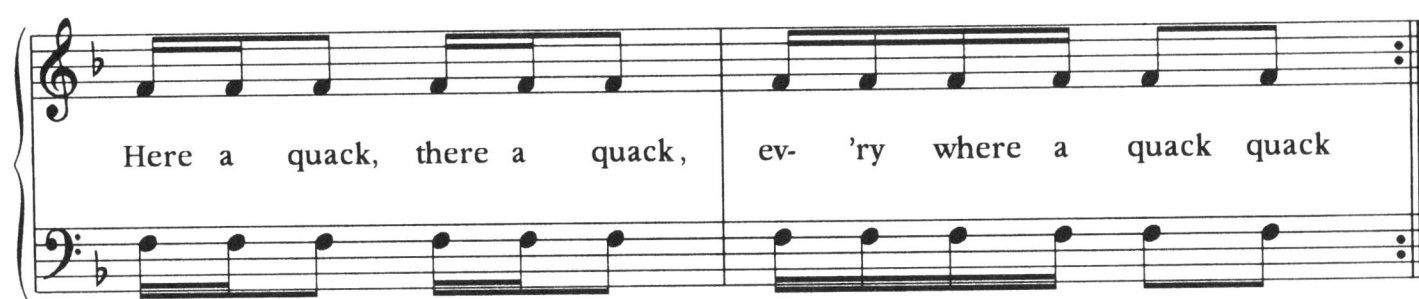

Verses:

1. Duck: quack-quack
2. Chick: chick, chick
3. Cow: moo, moo
4. Dog: bow-wow
5. Pig: oink, oink
6. Rooster: cock-a-doodle
7. Turkey: gobble, gobble
8. Cat: meow, meow
9. Horse: neigh neigh
10. Donkey: he-haw

Three Blind Mice

Mother Goose

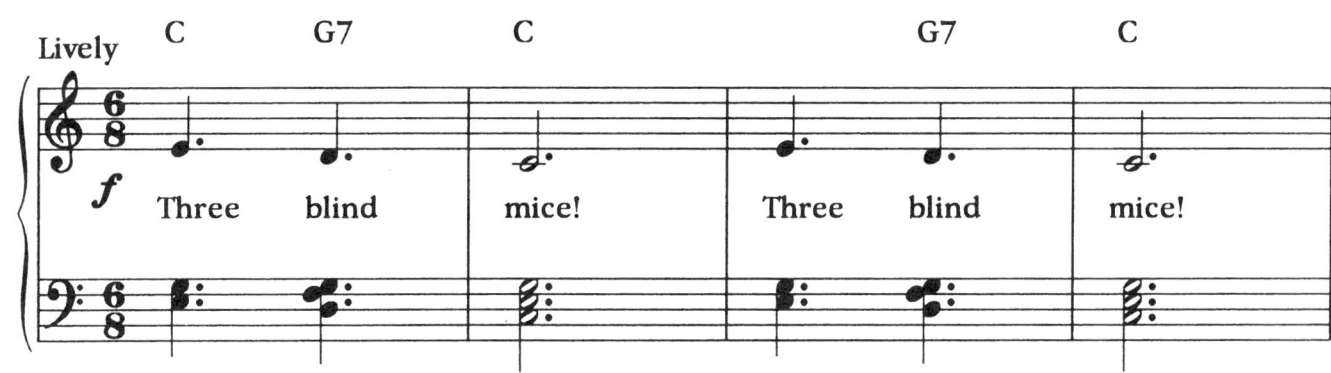

Three blind mice! Three blind mice!

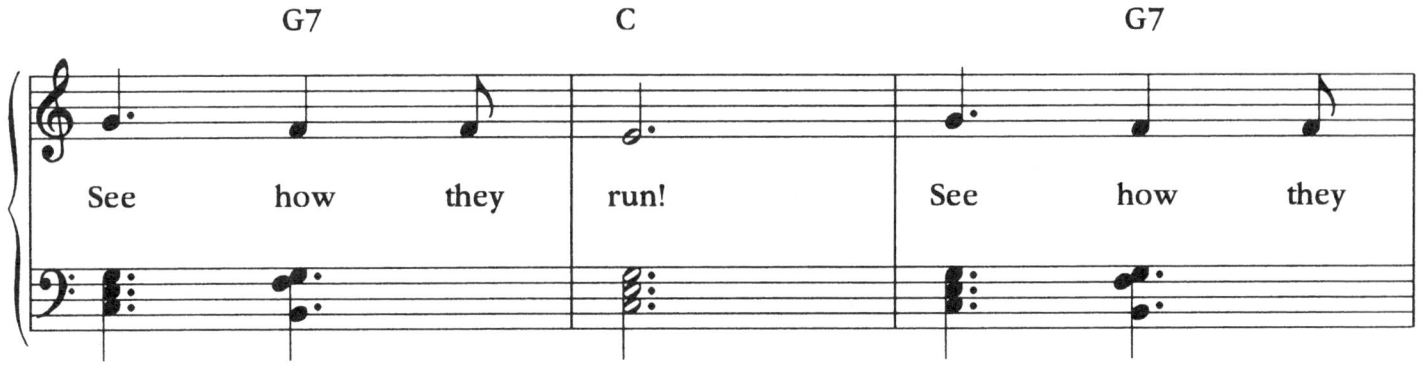

See how they run! See how they

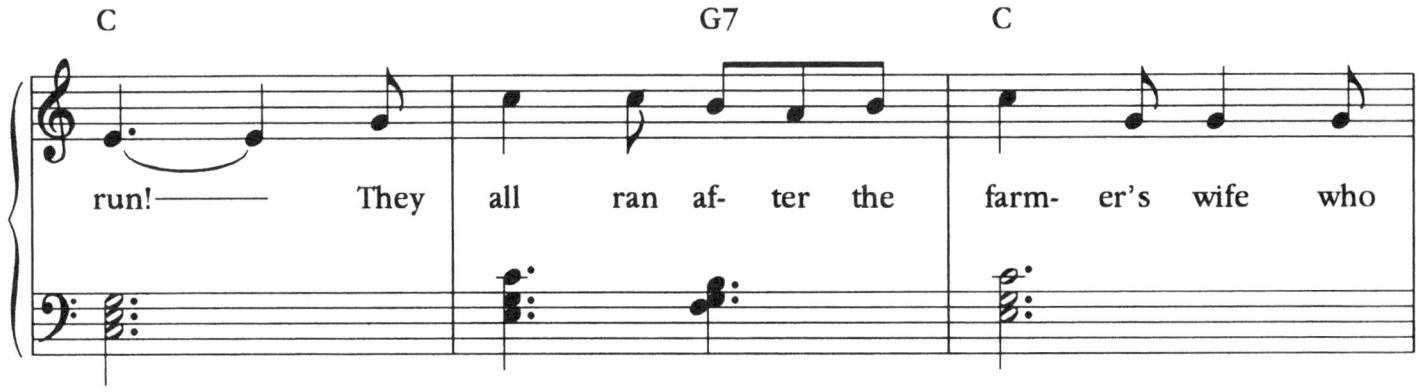

run!——— They all ran af- ter the farm- er's wife who

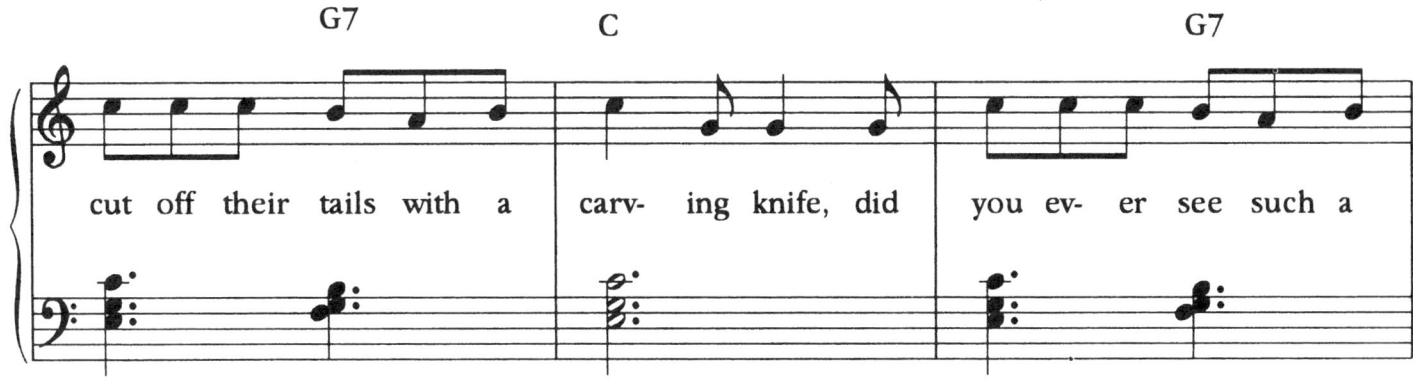

cut off their tails with a carv- ing knife, did you ev- er see such a

sight   in   your   life,   as   three   blind   mice?

Frere Jacques (Brother John)

Fr: Fre - re Jac - ques,   Fre - re Jac - ques,   dor -mez vous?
Eng: Are you sleep- ing?   Are you sleep- ing?   Broth- er John?

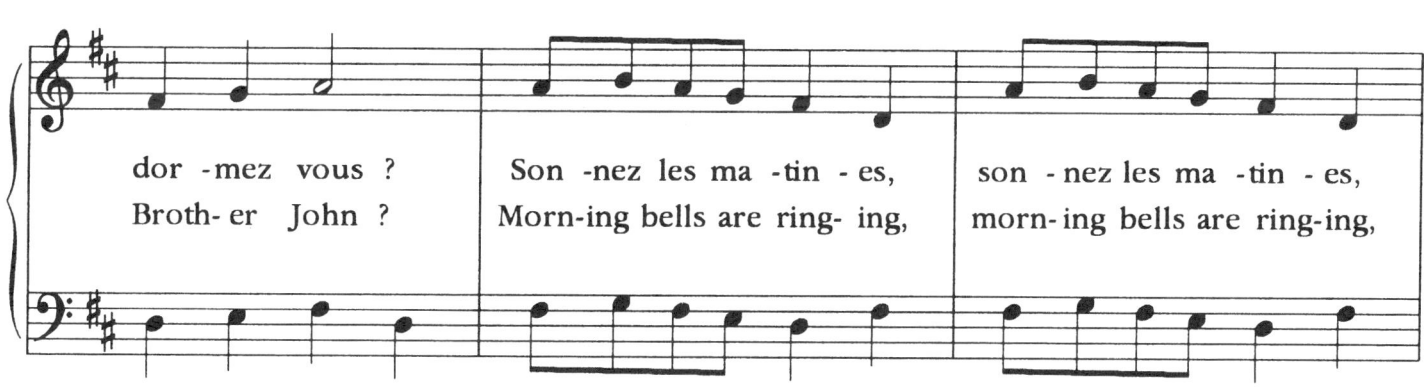

dor -mez vous ?   Son -nez les ma -tin - es,   son - nez les ma -tin - es,
Broth- er John ?   Morn-ing bells are ring- ing,   morn-ing bells are ring-ing,

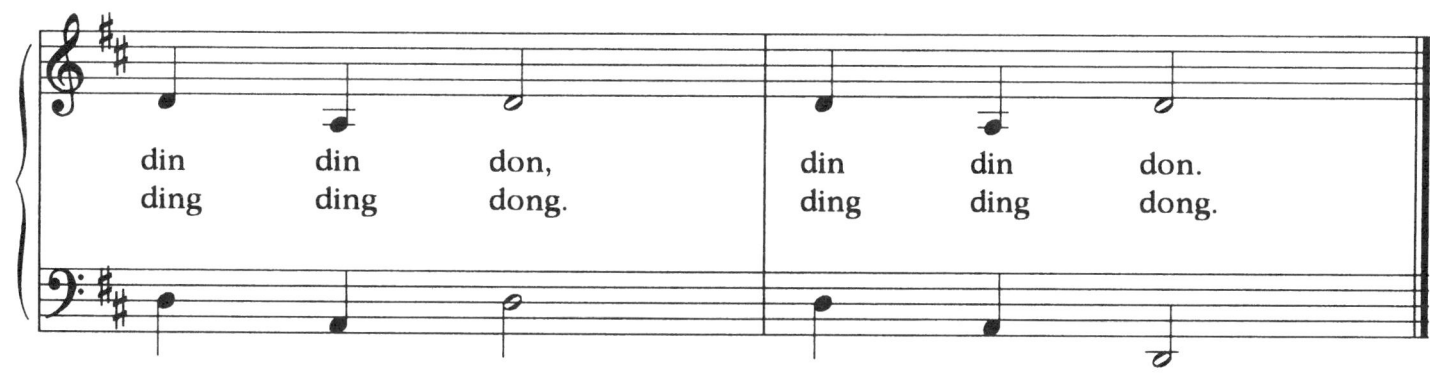

din   din   don,   din   din   don.
ding   ding   dong.   ding   ding   dong.

Jack And Jill

2. Up Jack got and home did trot
   As fast as he could caper;
   Went to bed to mend his head
   With vinegar and brown paper.

3. Jill came in, how she did grin
   To see Jack's paper plaster;
   Mother, vexed, did whip her next
   For causing Jack's disaster.

Little Boy Blue

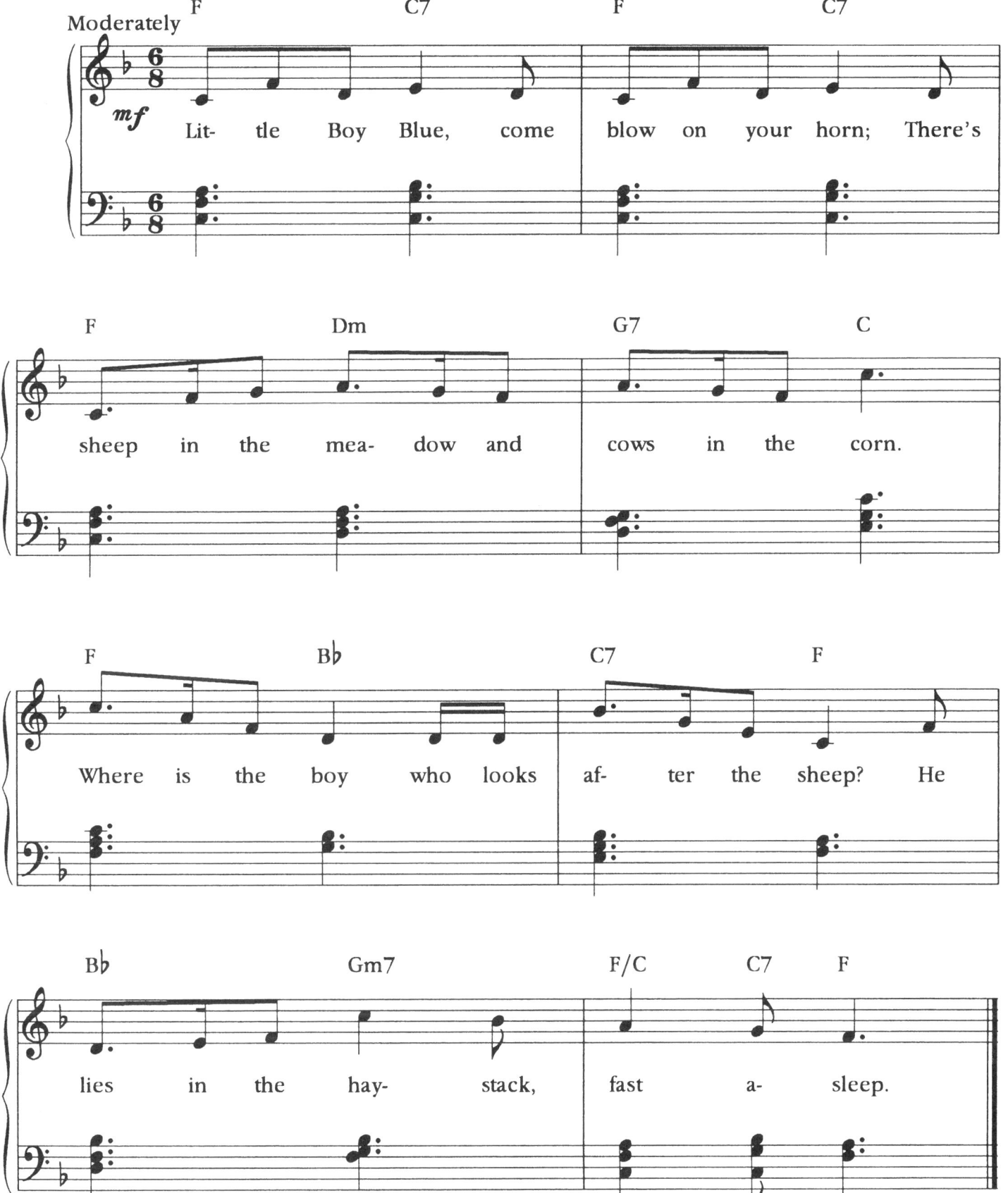

Little Bo-Peep

John Jacob Jingleheimer Schmidt

Traditional

The Animal Fair

Lively

Traditional

I went to the an- i- mal fair, —— the

birds and bees were there. —— The old ba- boon by the

light of the moon was comb- ing his au- burn hair. —— The

mon- key he got drunk—— and sat on the el- e- phants'

trunk. —— The el- e- phant sneezed and fell on his knees and

what be- came of the monk, the monk, the monk the monk?

The Farmer In The Dell

Traditional

Allegro

The far -mer in the dell, ── the far - mer in the dell,

mf

hi, ho, the der - ry - o, the far - mer in the dell. ──

2. The farmer takes a wife, etc.

3. The wife takes a child, etc.

4. The child takes a nurse, etc.

5. The nurse takes a dog, etc.

6. The dog takes a cat, etc.

7. The cat takes a rat, etc.

8. The rat takes the cheese, etc.

9. The cheese stands alone, etc.

Pease Porridge Hot

Traditional

Little Miss Muffet

Allegretto

D7   G

mf

Lit- tle Miss Muf- fet   sat on a tuf- fet

D7   G   D7

eat - ing some curds and   whey.———— There   came a big spi- der who

G   D7   G

sat down be- side her and   fright- ened Miss Muf -fet a-   way.————

Little Jack Horner

Mother Goose

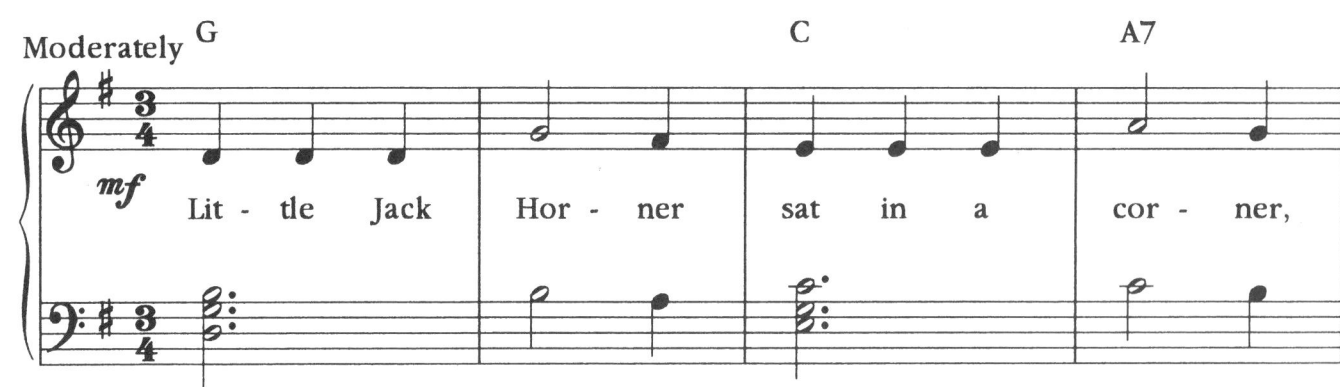

Little Jack Horner sat in a corner,

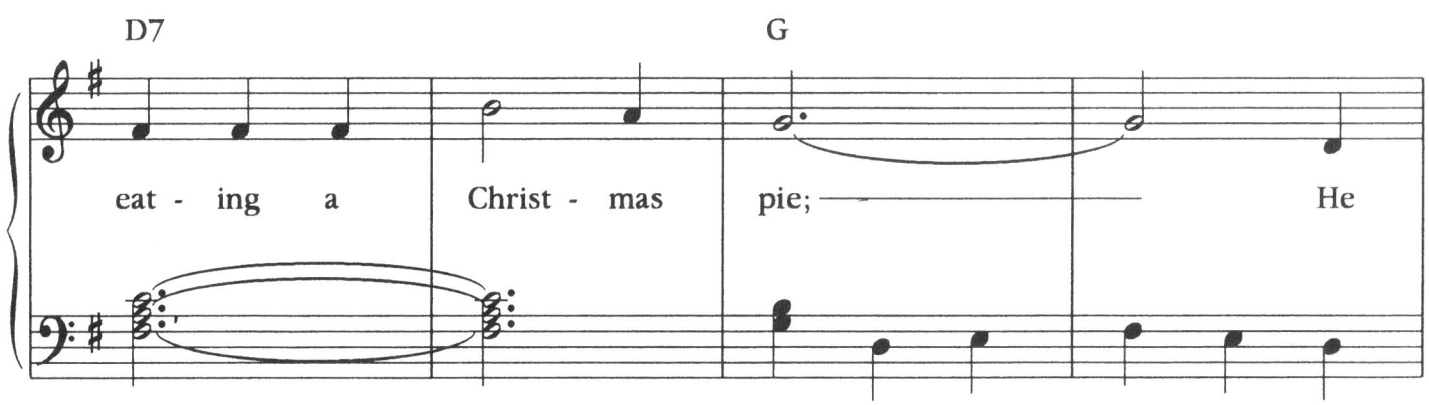

eating a Christmas pie; He

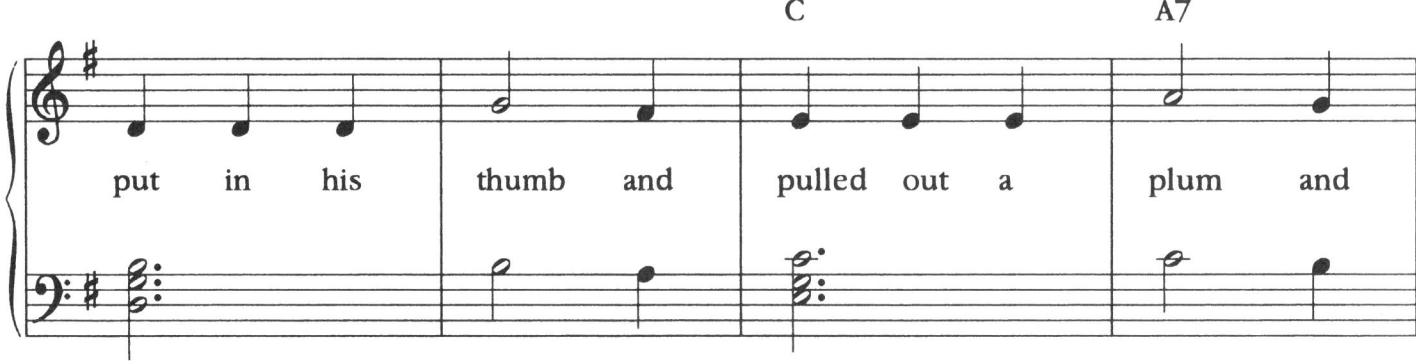

put in his thumb and pulled out a plum and

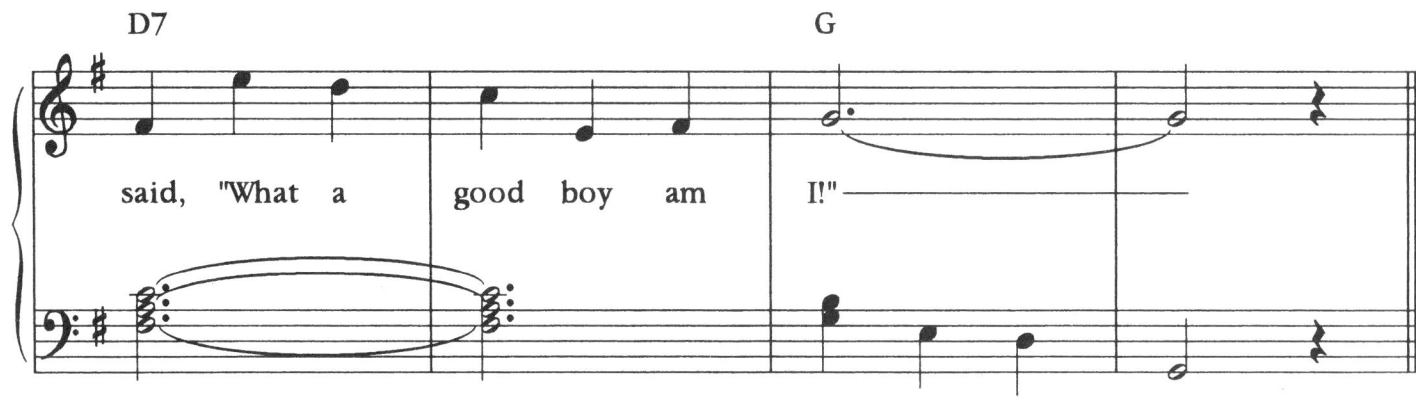

said, "What a good boy am I!"

The Mulberry Bush

Mother Goose

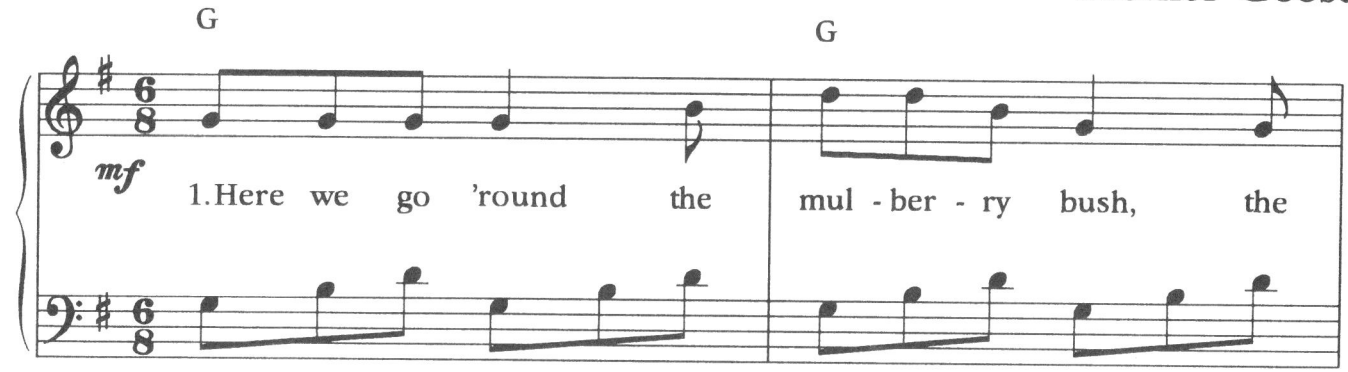

1.Here we go 'round the mul-ber-ry bush, the

mul-ber-ry bush, the mul-ber-ry bush. Here we go 'round the

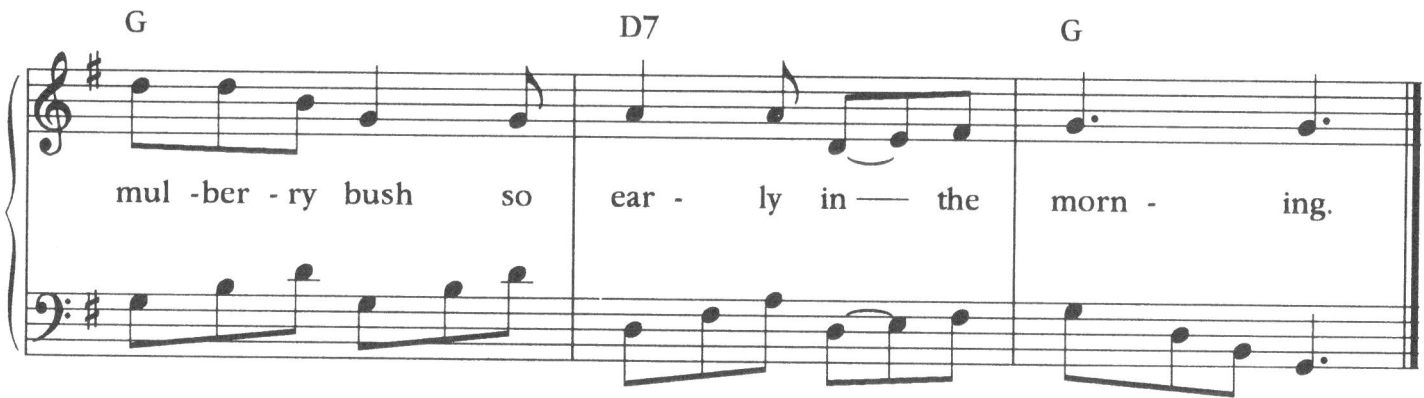

mul-ber-ry bush so ear-ly in — the morn- ing.

2. This is the way we wash our clothes,
   We wash our clothes, we wash our clothes.
   This is the way we wash our clothes,
   So early Monday morning.

3. This is the way we iron our clothes,
   We iron our clothes, we iron our clothes.
   This is the way we iron our clothes,
   So early Tuesday morning.

4. This is the way we scrub the floor,
   We scrub the floor, we scrub the floor.
   This is the way we scrub the floor,
   So early Wednesday morning.

5. This is the way we mend our clothes,
   We mend our clothes, we mend our clothes.
   This is the way we mend our clothes,
   So early Thursday morning.

6. This is the way we sweep the house,
   We sweep the house, we sweep the house.
   This is the way we seep the house,
   So early Friday morning.

7. This is the way we bake our bread,
   We bake our bread, we bake our bread.
   This is the way we bake our bread,
   So early Saturday morning.

8. This is the way we go to church,
   We go to church, we go to church.
   This is the way we go to church,
   So early Sunday morning.

Old Gray Mare

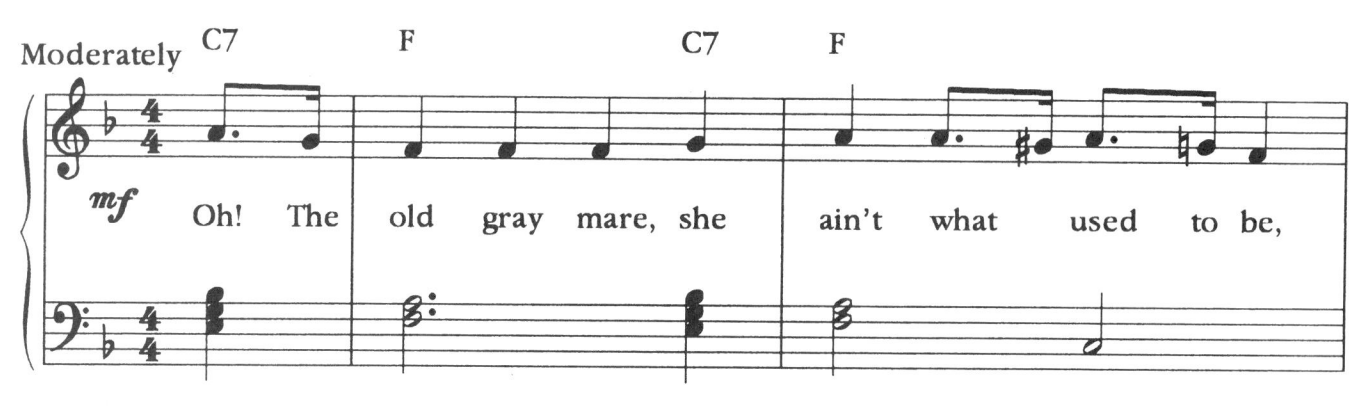

Oh! The old gray mare, she ain't what used to be,

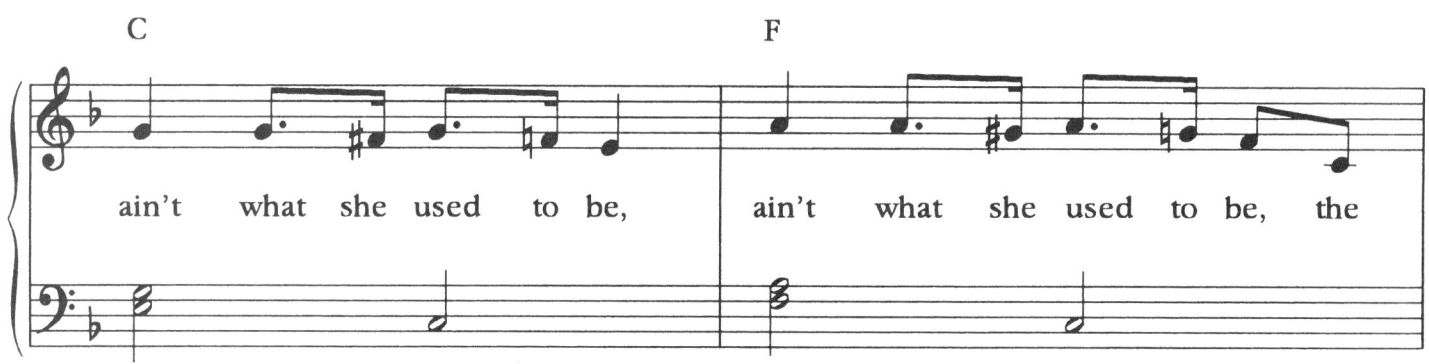

ain't what she used to be, ain't what she used to be, the

old gray mare, she ain't what she used to be,

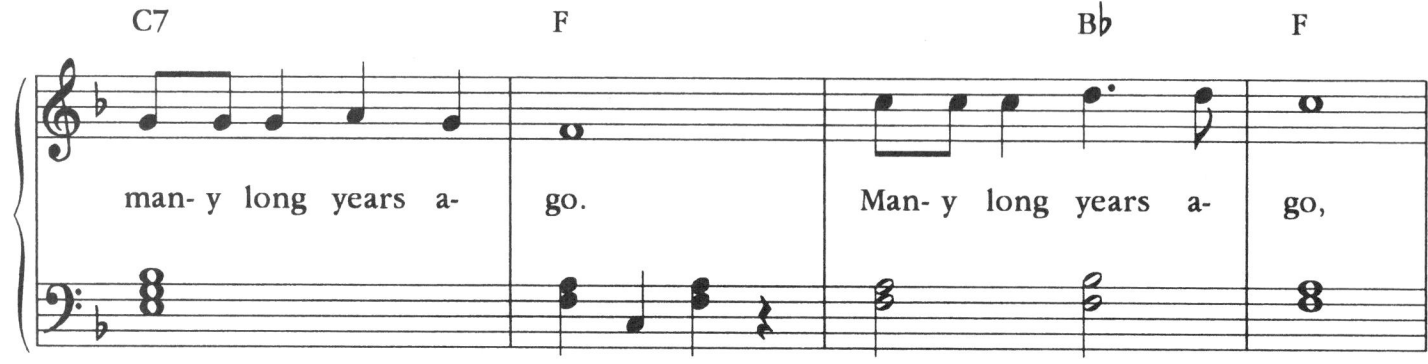

man- y long years a- go. Man- y long years a- go,

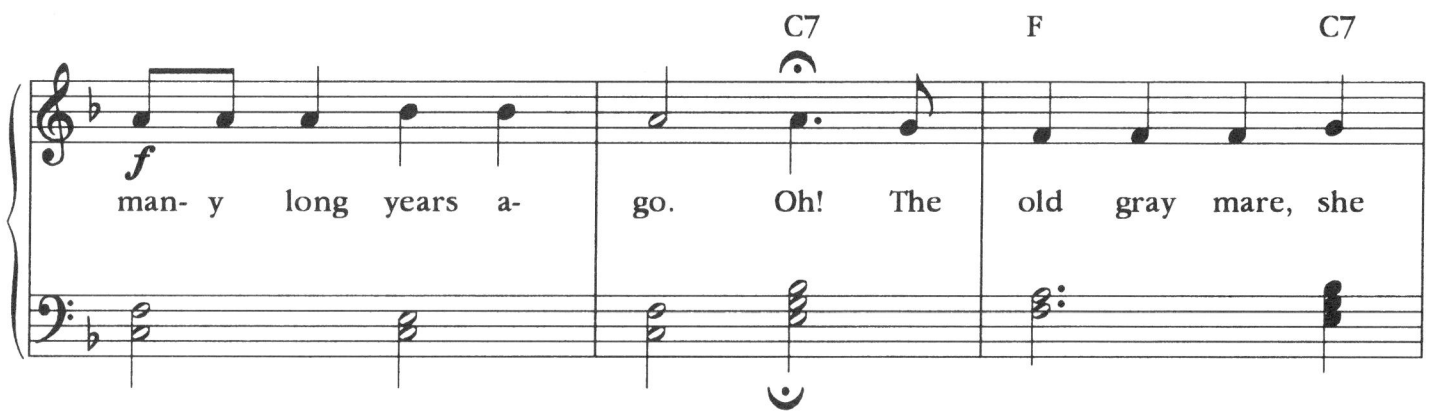

man-y long years a- go. Oh! The old gray mare, she

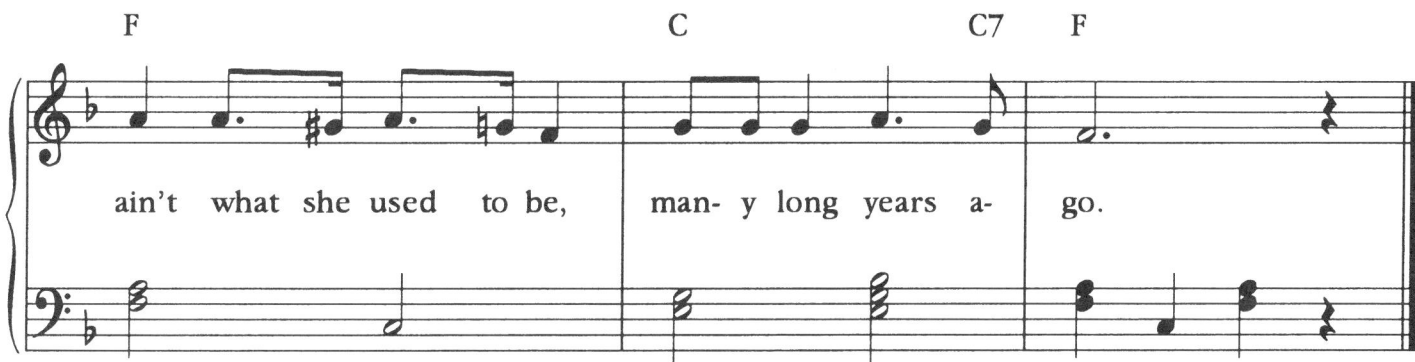

ain't what she used to be, man-y long years a- go.

It's Raining, It's Pouring

German Folk Song

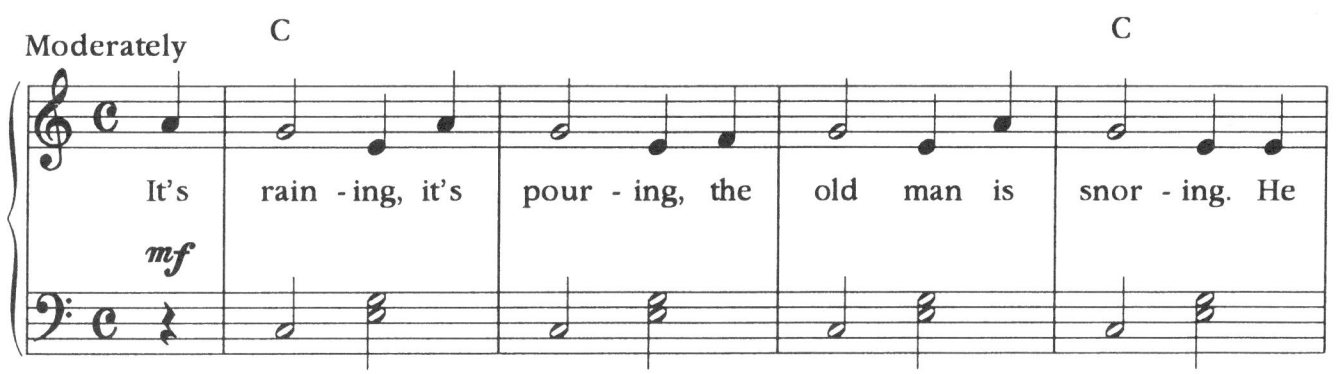

It's rain - ing, it's pour - ing, the old man is snor - ing. He

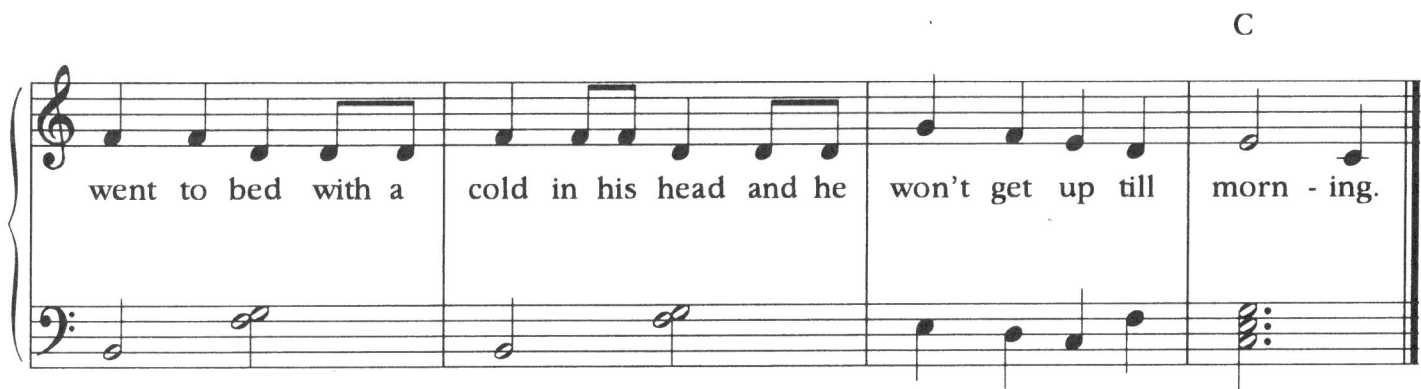

went to bed with a cold in his head and he won't get up till morn - ing.

Alouette (The Lark)

French Folk Song

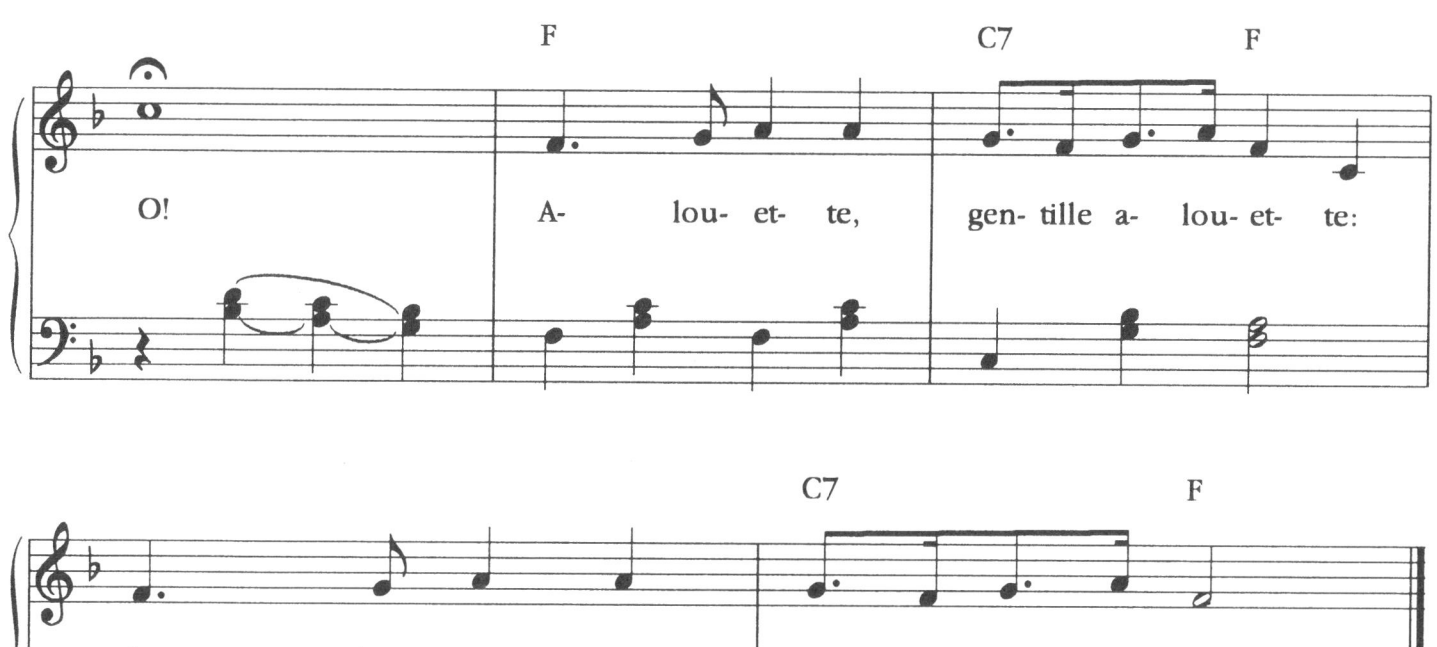

O! A- lou- et- te, gen- tille a- lou- et- te:

A- lou- et- te, je te plu- me- rai.

London Bridge

Traditional

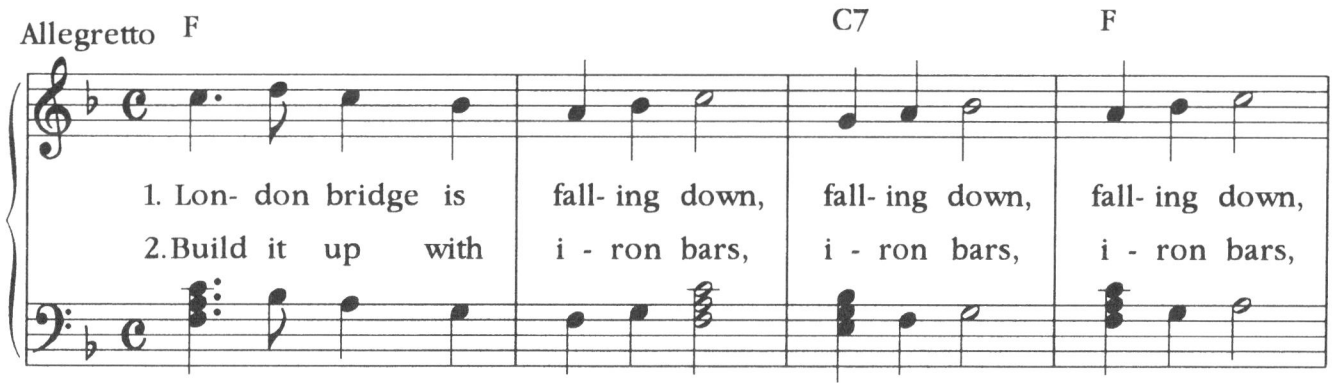

Allegretto

1. Lon- don bridge is fall- ing down, fall- ing down, fall- ing down,
2. Build it up with i - ron bars, i - ron bars, i - ron bars,

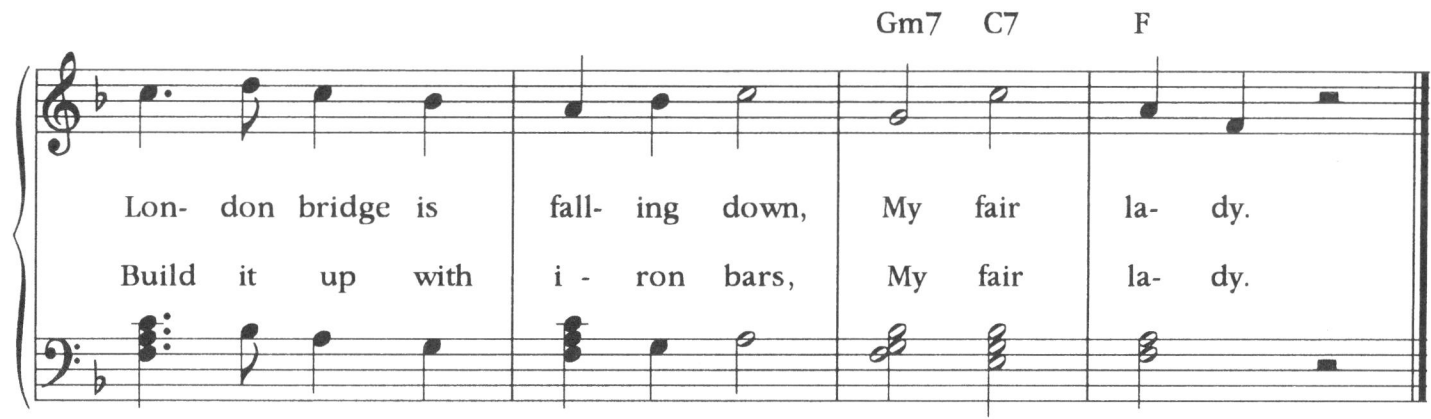

Lon- don bridge is fall- ing down, My fair la- dy.

Build it up with i - ron bars, My fair la- dy.

Where, Oh Where Has My Little Dog Gone?

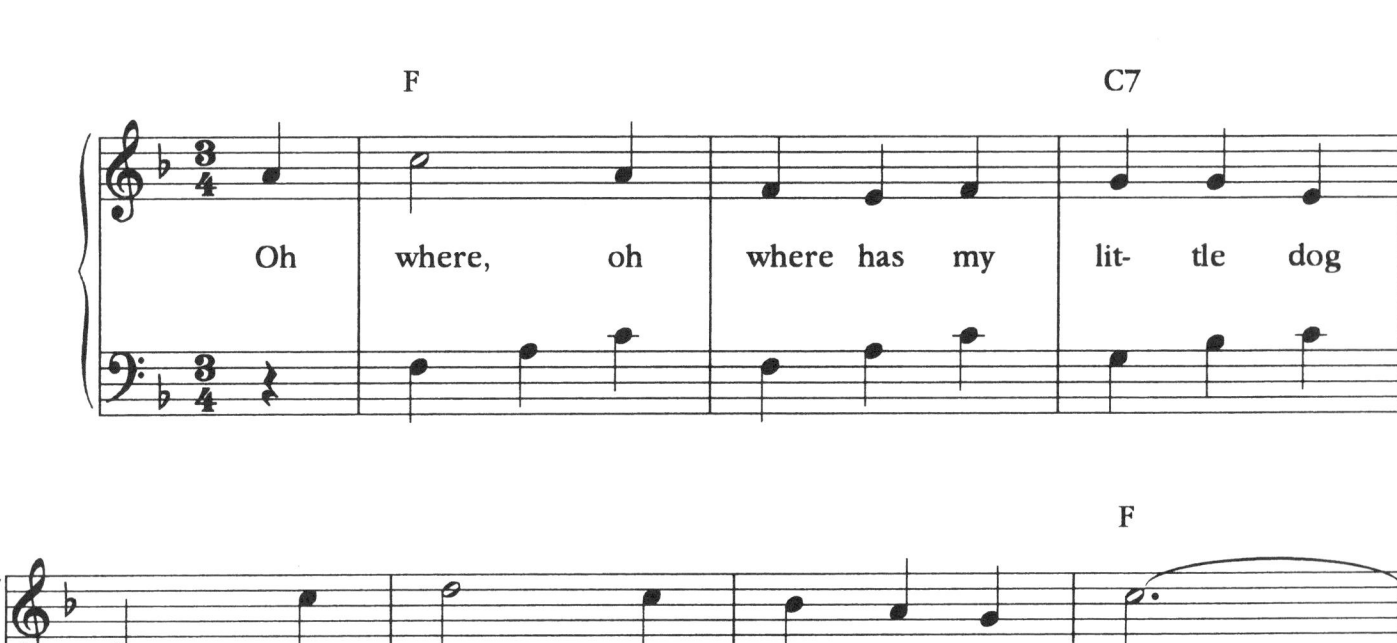

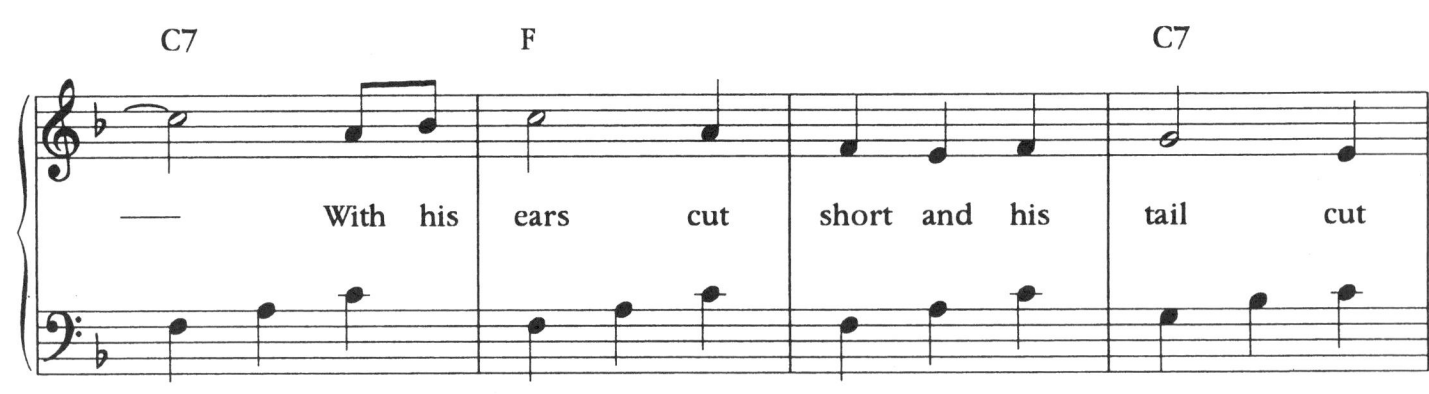

The Muffin Man

Traditional

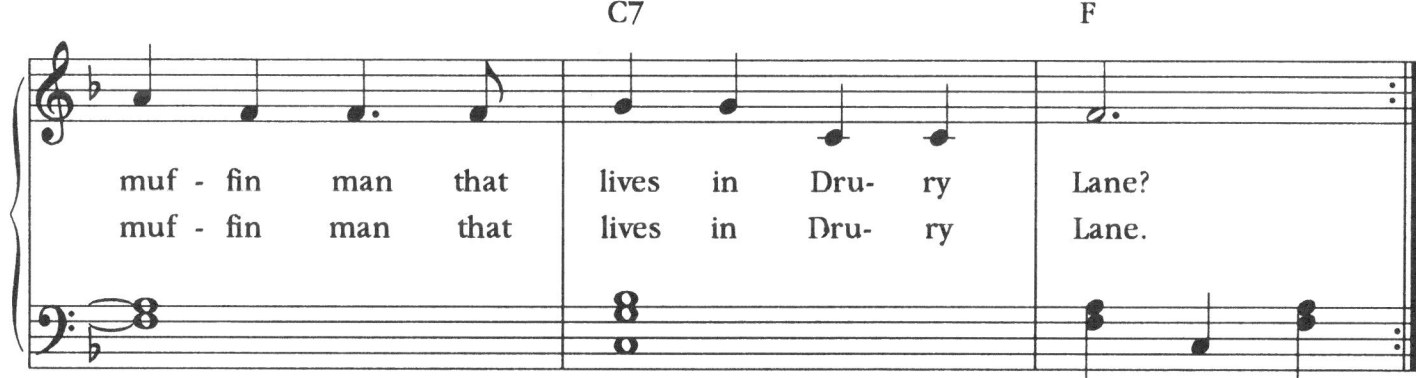

Oh Dear! What Can The Matter Be ?

Scottish Folk Song

pro- mised to buy me a bas- ket of po- sies, a

Em · A7 · A7

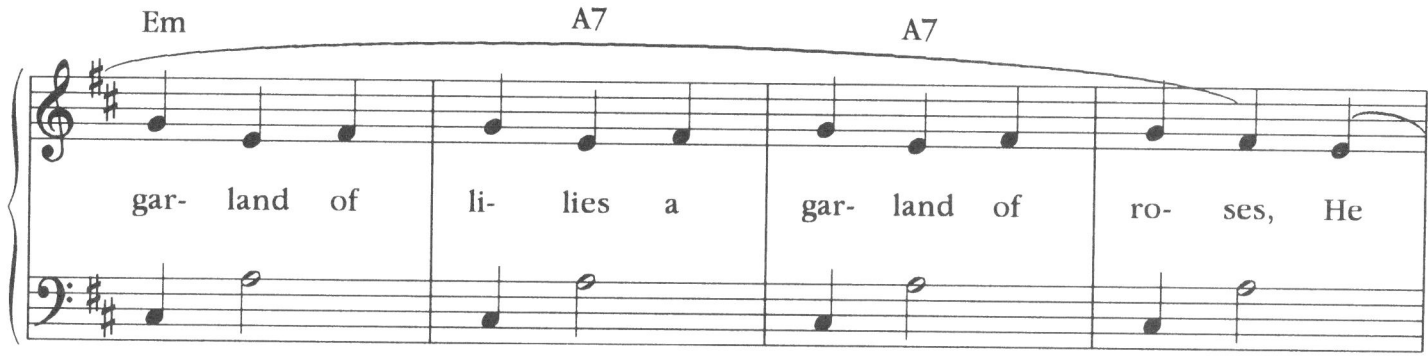

gar- land of li- lies a gar- land of ro- ses, He

D

pro- mised to buy me a bunch of blue rib- bons to

Em · A7 · D

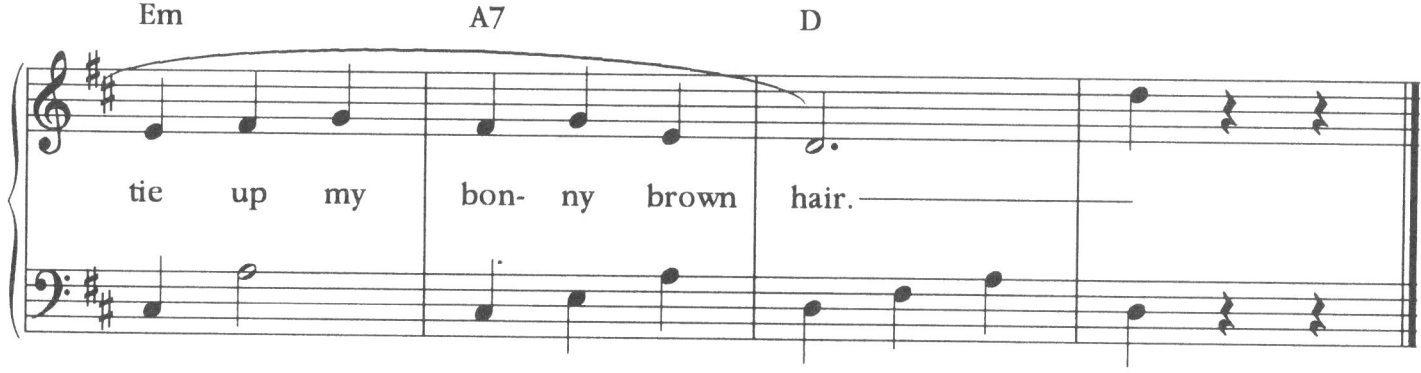

tie up my bon- ny brown hair.

B-I-N-G-O

Traditional

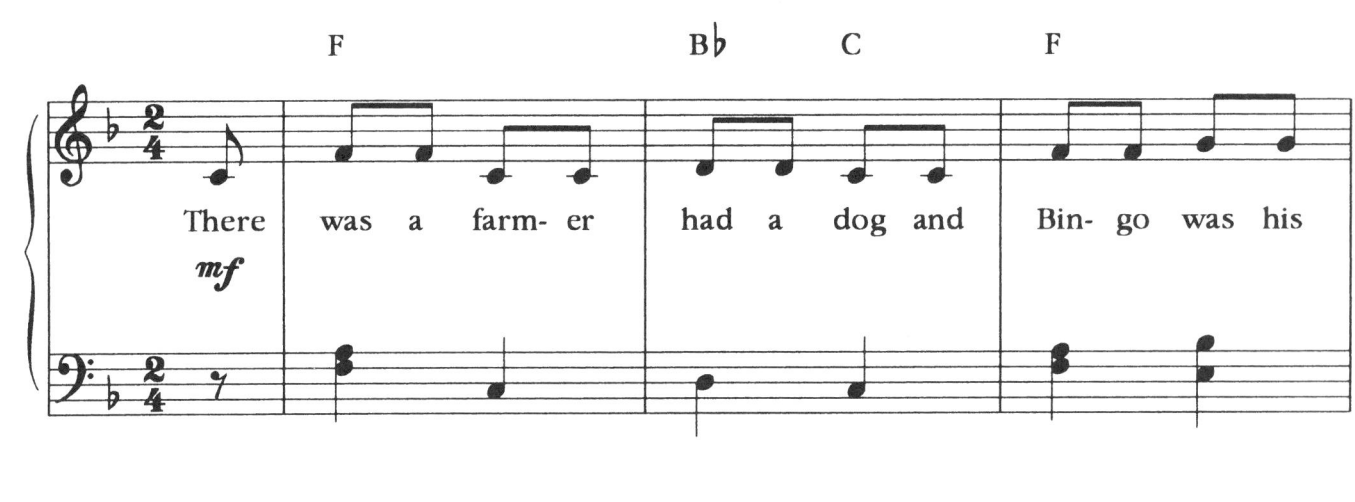

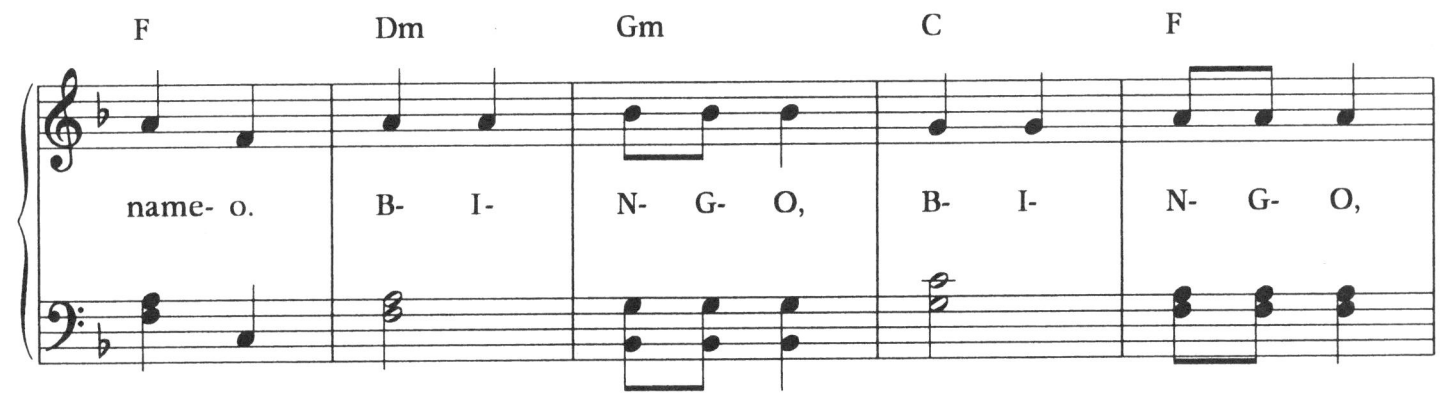

Ring Around The Rosy

Traditional

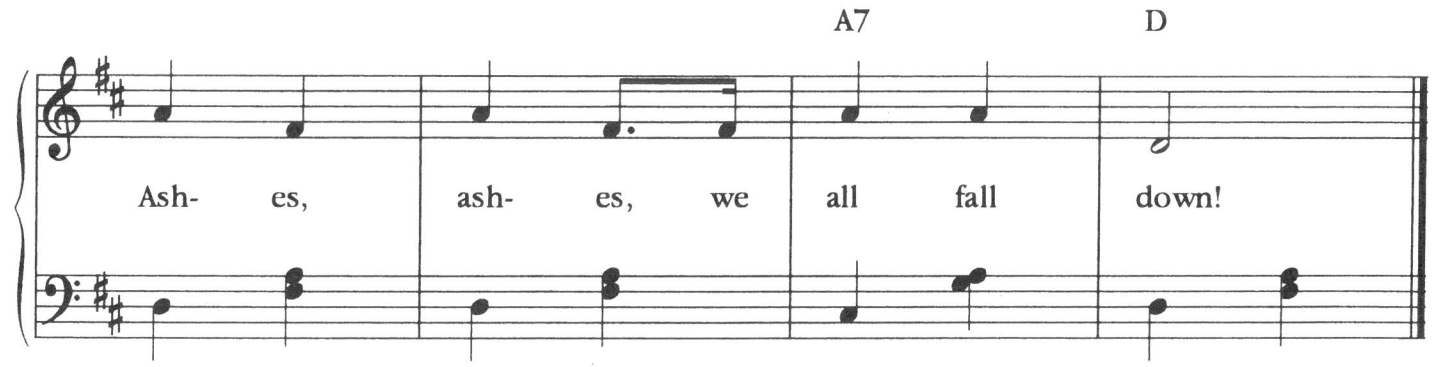

Old King Cole

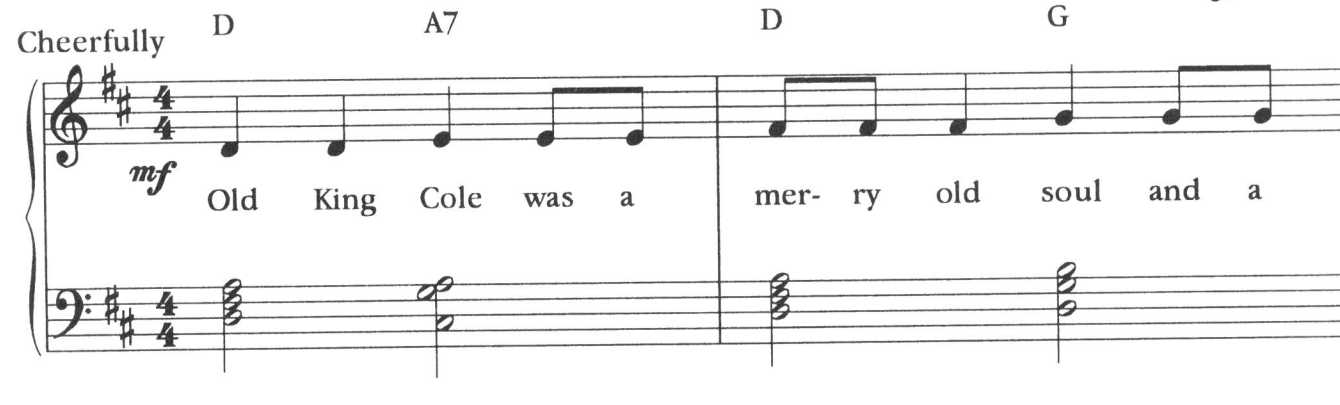

Cheerfully

Old King Cole was a mer- ry old soul and a

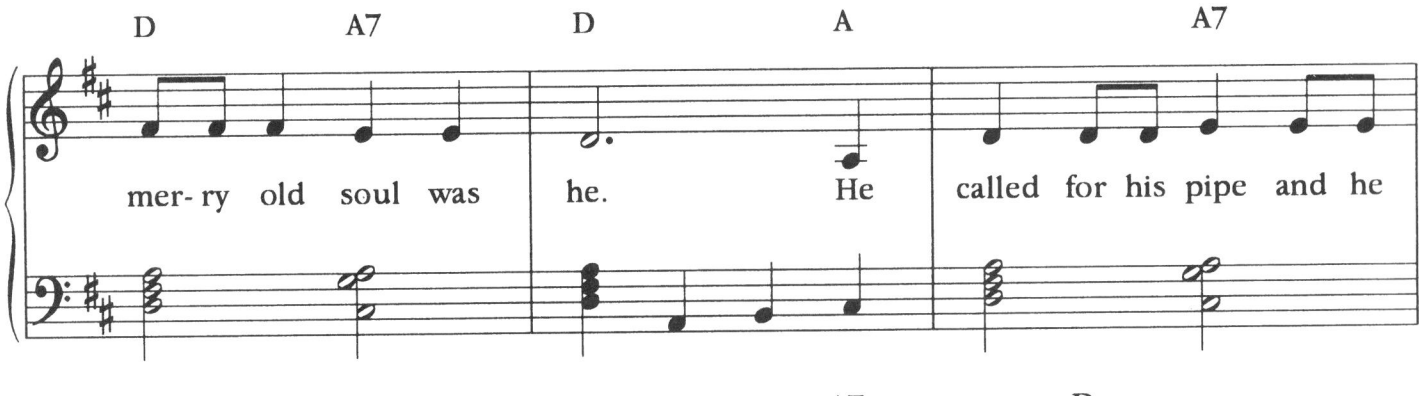

mer- ry old soul was he. He called for his pipe and he

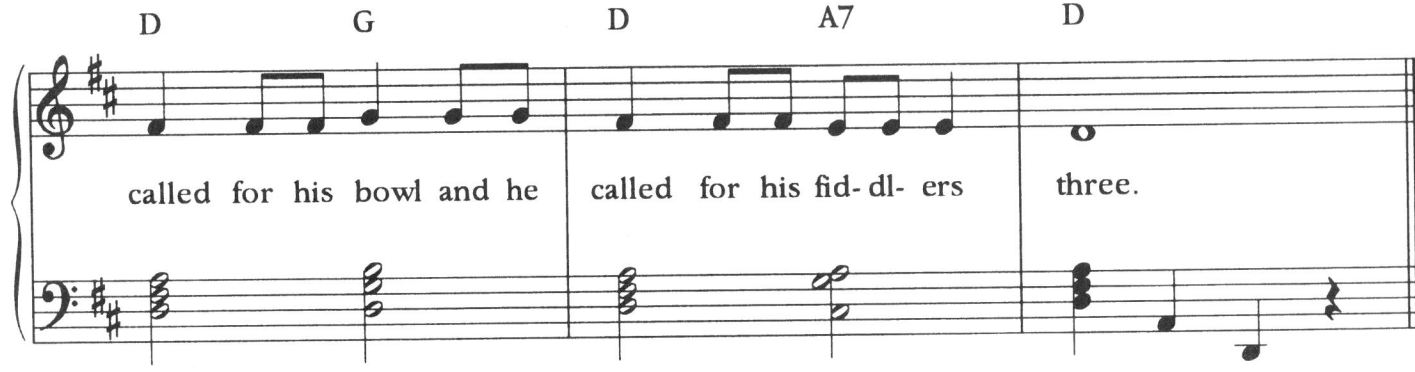

called for his bowl and he called for his fid- dl- ers three.

Pat-A-Cake

Polly Wolly Doodle

Traditional

Brightly   F

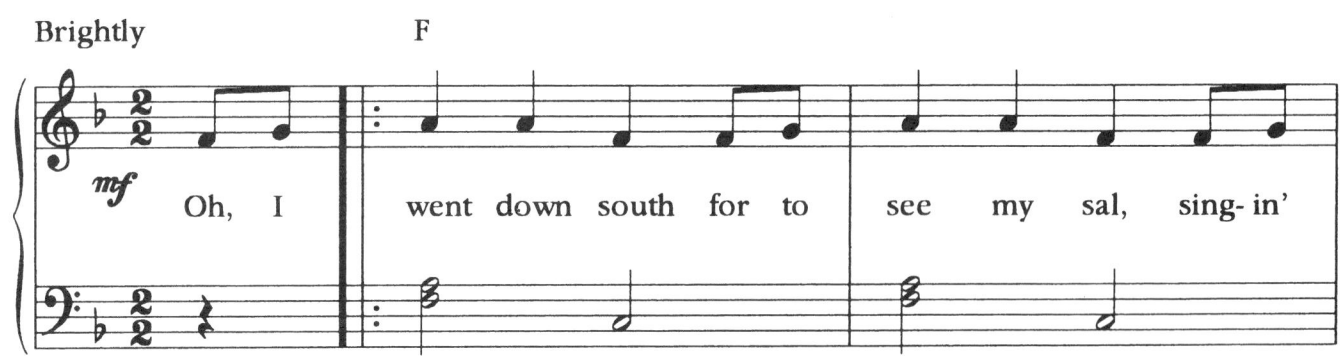

Oh, I   went down south for to   see my sal, sing-in'

C7

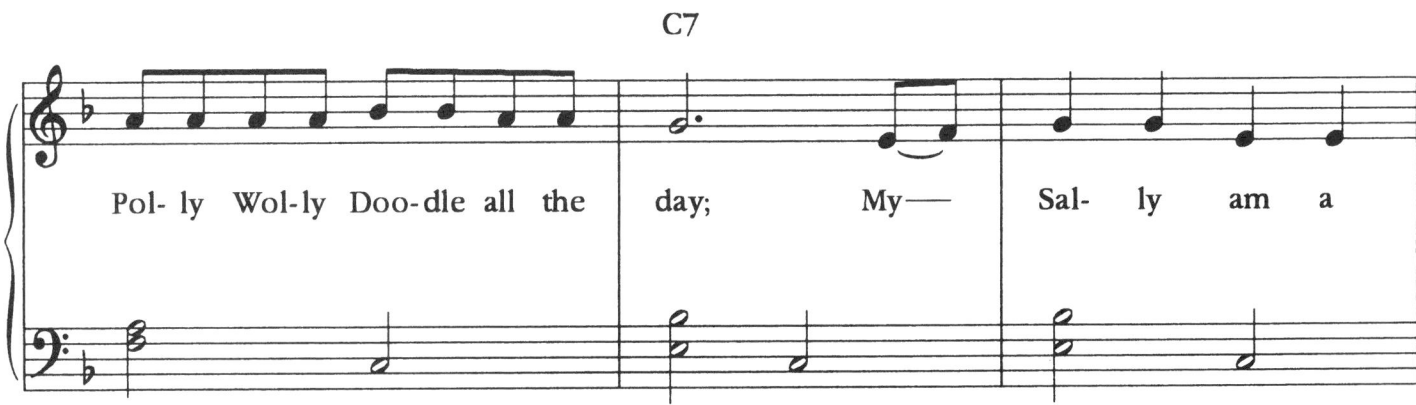

Pol-ly Wol-ly Doo-dle all the   day;   My——   Sal-ly am a

spunk-y gal, sing-in'   Pol-ly Wol ly Doo-dle all the   day.   Fare thee

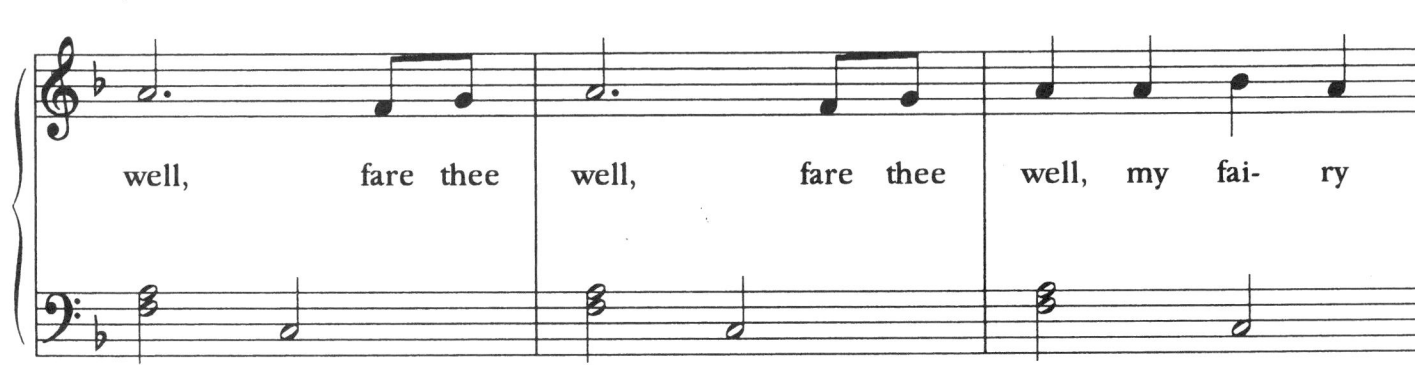

well,   fare thee well,   fare thee well, my fai-ry

51

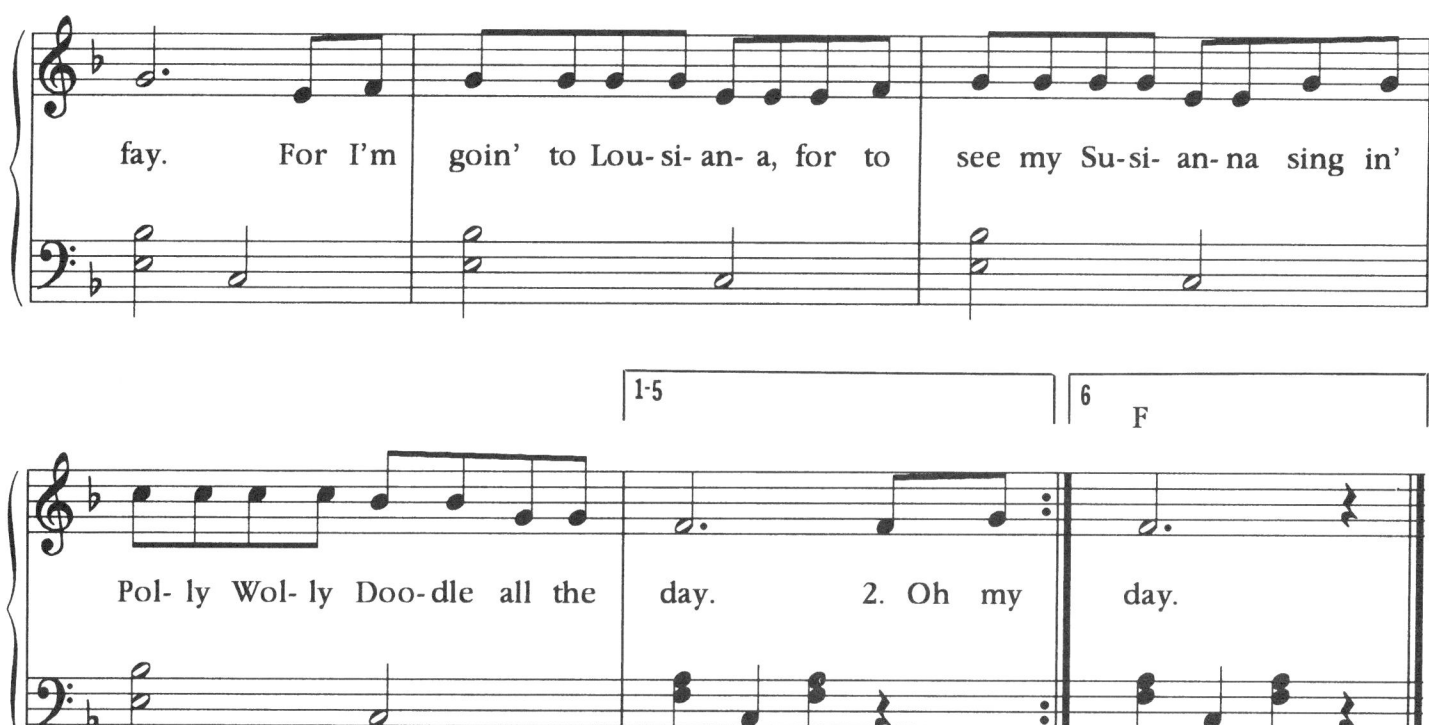

2. Sal she is a maiden fair,
   Singing polly wolly doodle all the day.
   With curly eyes and laughing hair,
   Singing polly wolly doodle all the day.
   Chorus:

3. Oh, a grasshopper sittin' on a railroad track,
   Singing polly-wolly-doodle all the day.
   A pickin' his teeth with a carpet tack,
   Singing polly-wolly-doodle all the day.
   Chorus:

4. Oh, I went to bed, but it wasn't no use
   Singing polly-wolly-doodle all the day.
   My feet stuck out like a chicken roost,
   Singing polly-wolly-doodle all the day.

   Chorus:

5. Behind the barn down on my knees,
   Singing polly-wolly doodle-all the day.
   I thought I heard a chicken sneeze,
   Singing polly-wolly-doodle all the day.
   Chorus:

6. He sneezed so hard with the whooping cough,
   Singing polly-wolly- doodle all the day.
   He sneezed his head and tail right off,
   Singing polly-wolly-doodle all the day.
   Chorus:

Baa, Baa Black Sheep

Traditional

Ten Little Indians

Traditional

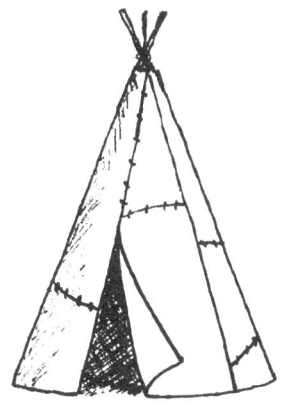

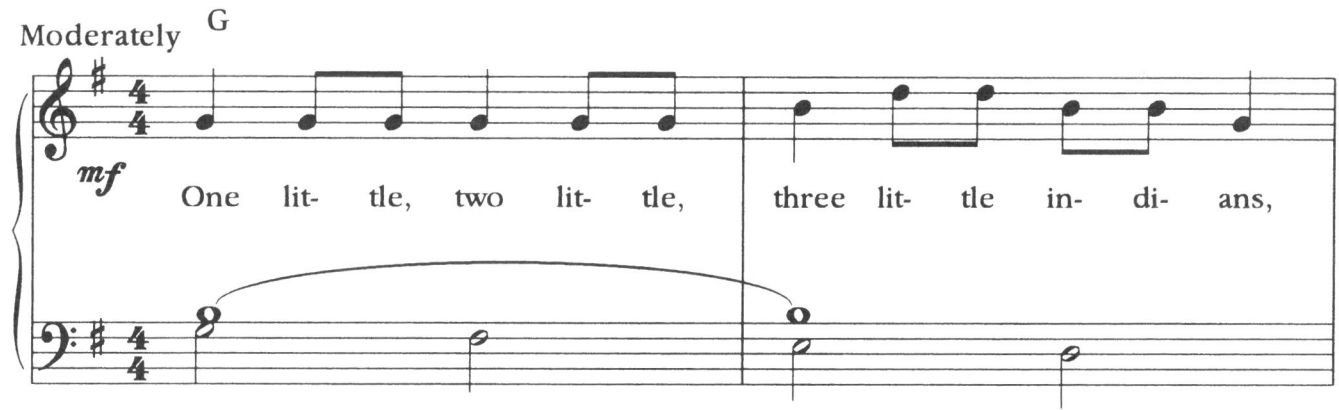

The Bear Went Over The Mountain

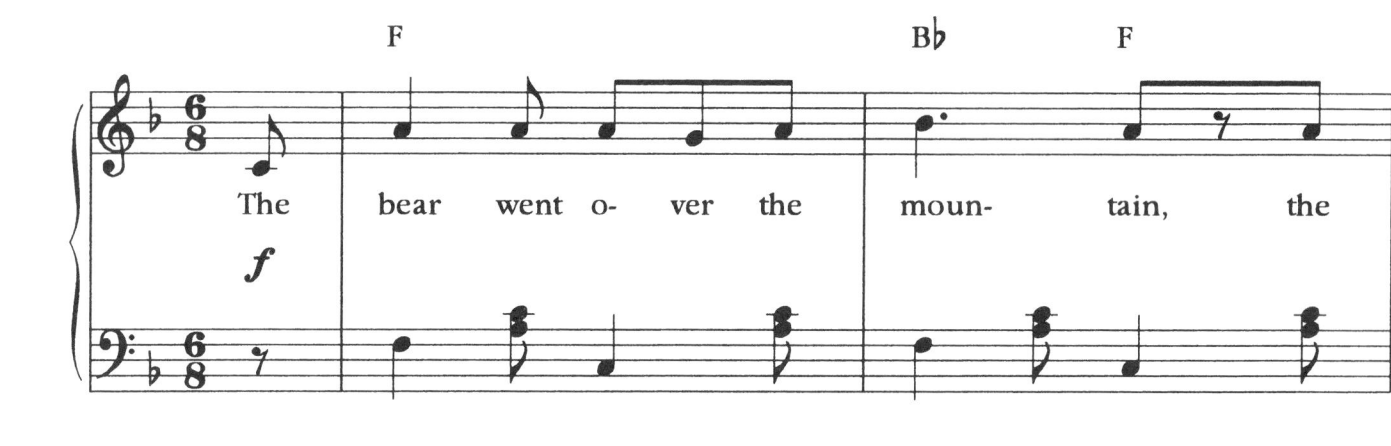

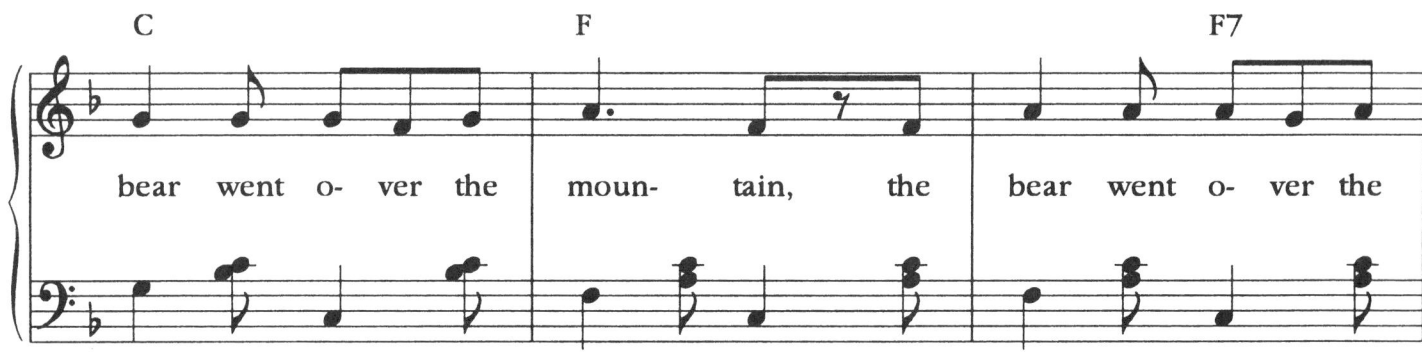

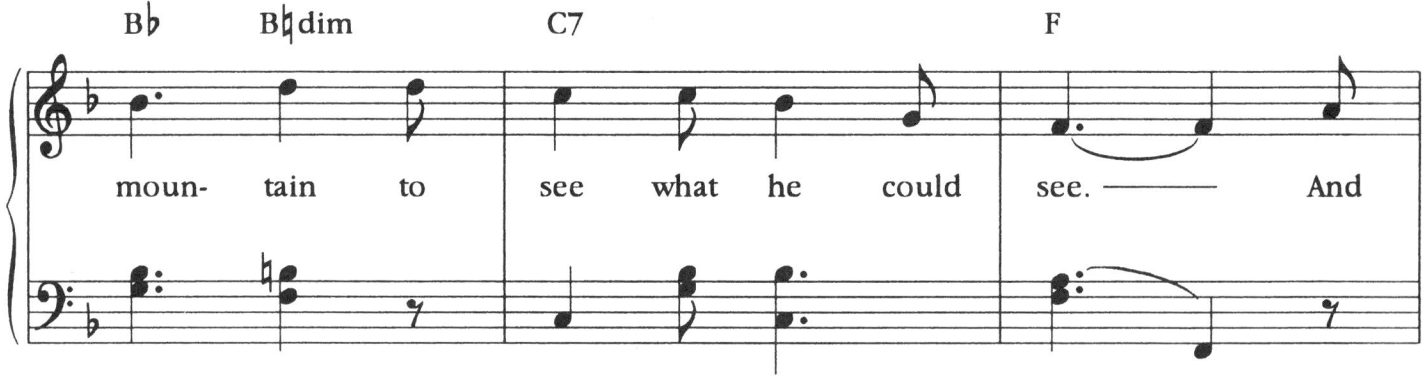

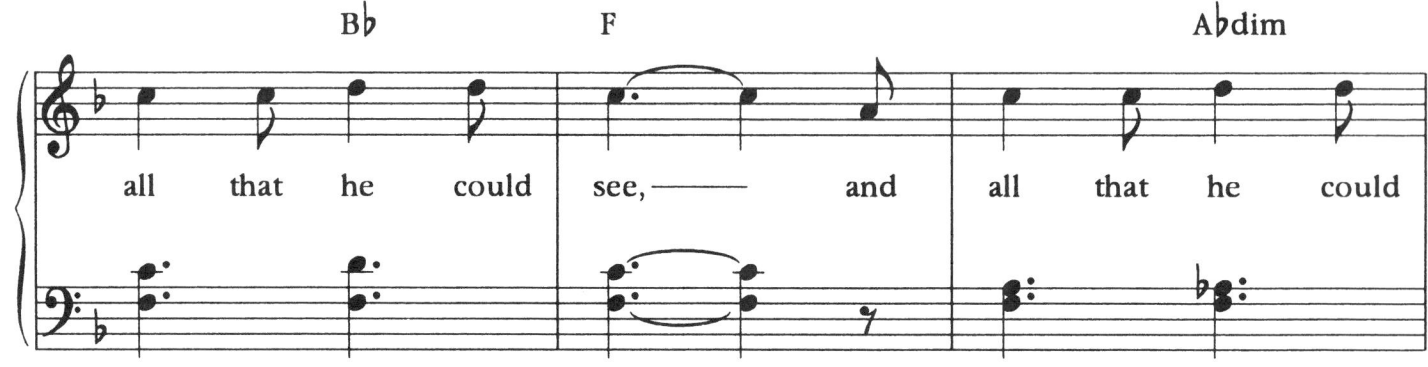

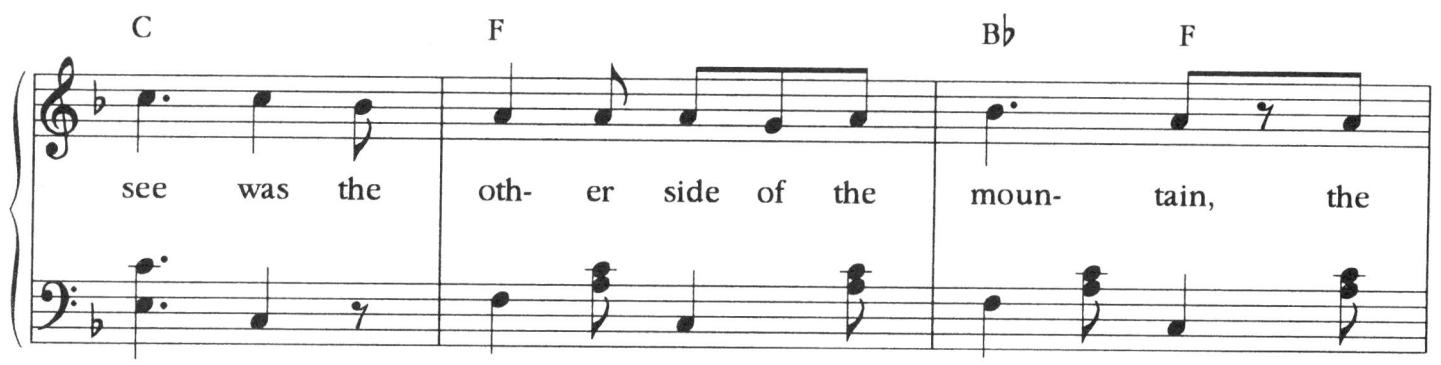

see was the oth- er side of the moun- tain, the

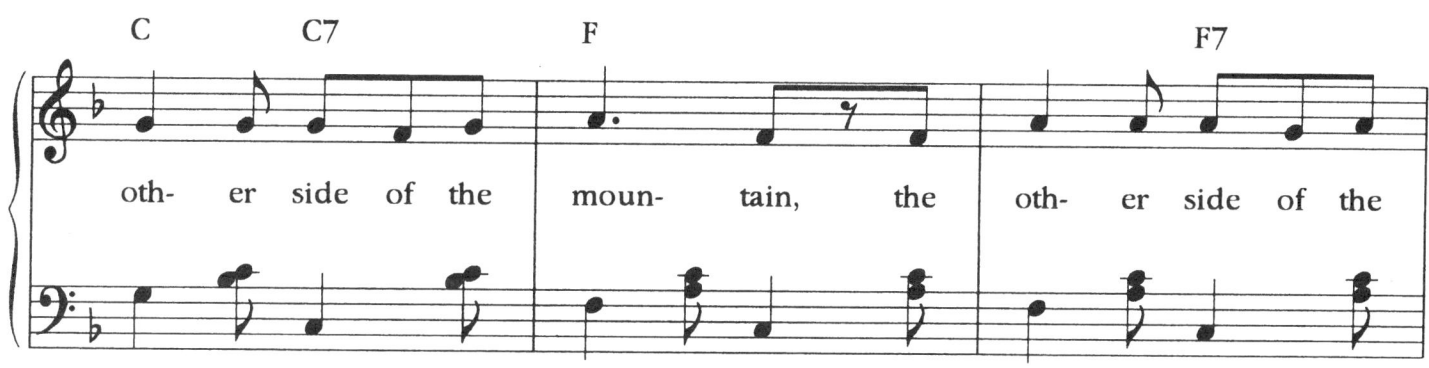

oth- er side of the moun- tain, the oth- er side of the

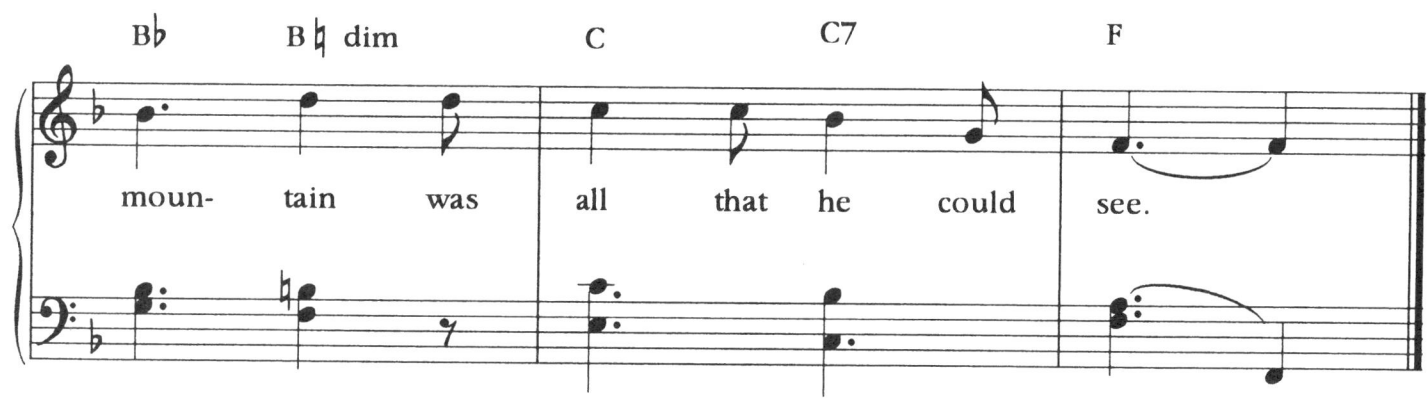

moun- tain was all that he could see.

Billy Boy

2. Did she bid you to come in,
   Billy Boy, Billy Boy?
   Did she bid you to come in,
   Charming Billy?
   Yes, she bade me to come in,
   There's a dimple in her chin,
   She's a young thing and can
   Not leave her mother.

3. Did she set for you a chair,
   Billy Boy, Billy Boy?
   Did she set for you a chair,
   Charming Billy?
   Yes, she set for me a chair,
   She has ringlets in her hair,
   She's a young thing and can
   Not leave her mother.

Pop! Goes The Weasel

Traditional

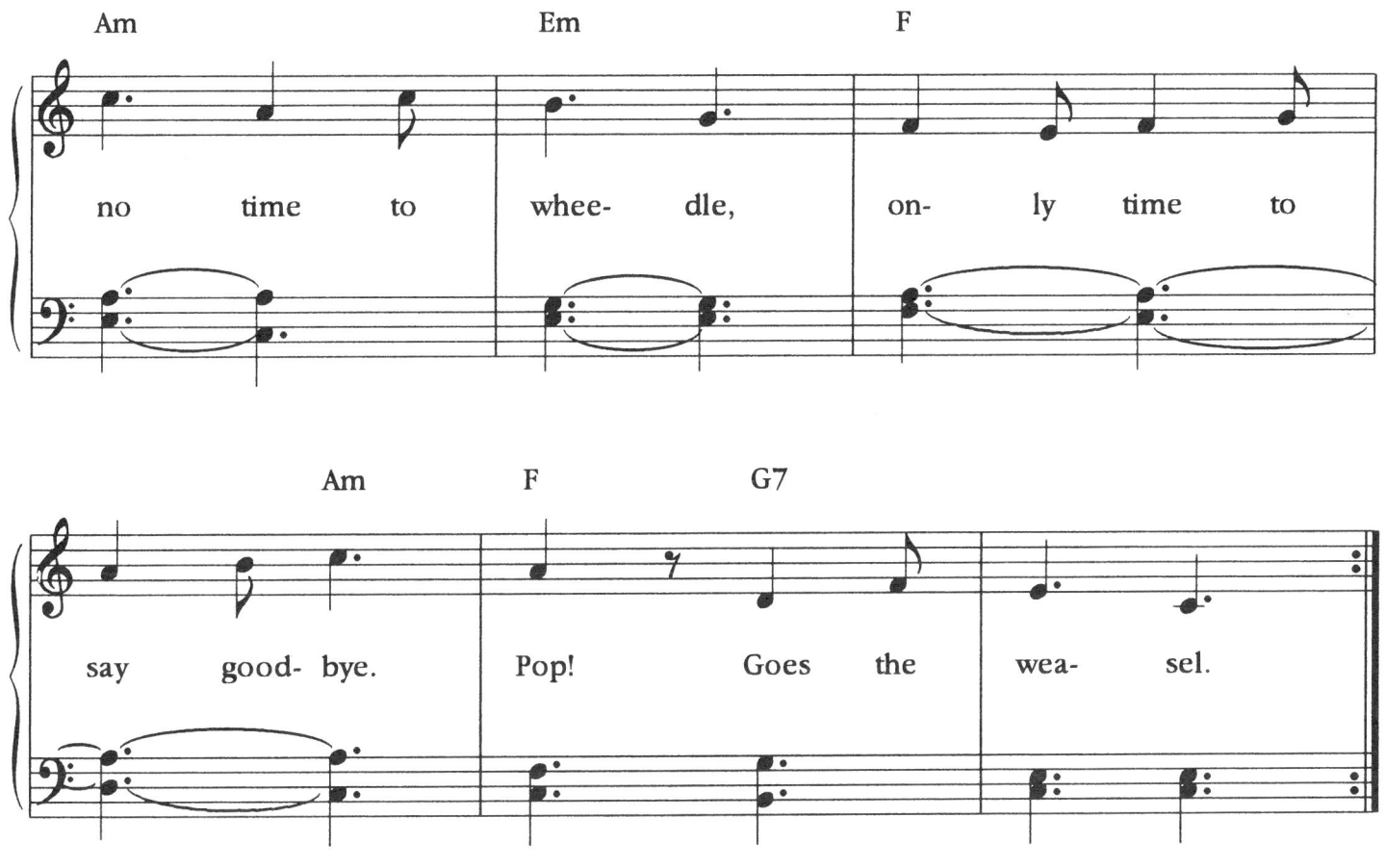

Am   Em   F

no time to   whee- dle,   on- ly time to

Am   F   G7

say   good- bye.   Pop!   Goes   the   wea- sel.

Row, Row, Row Your Boat

Traditional

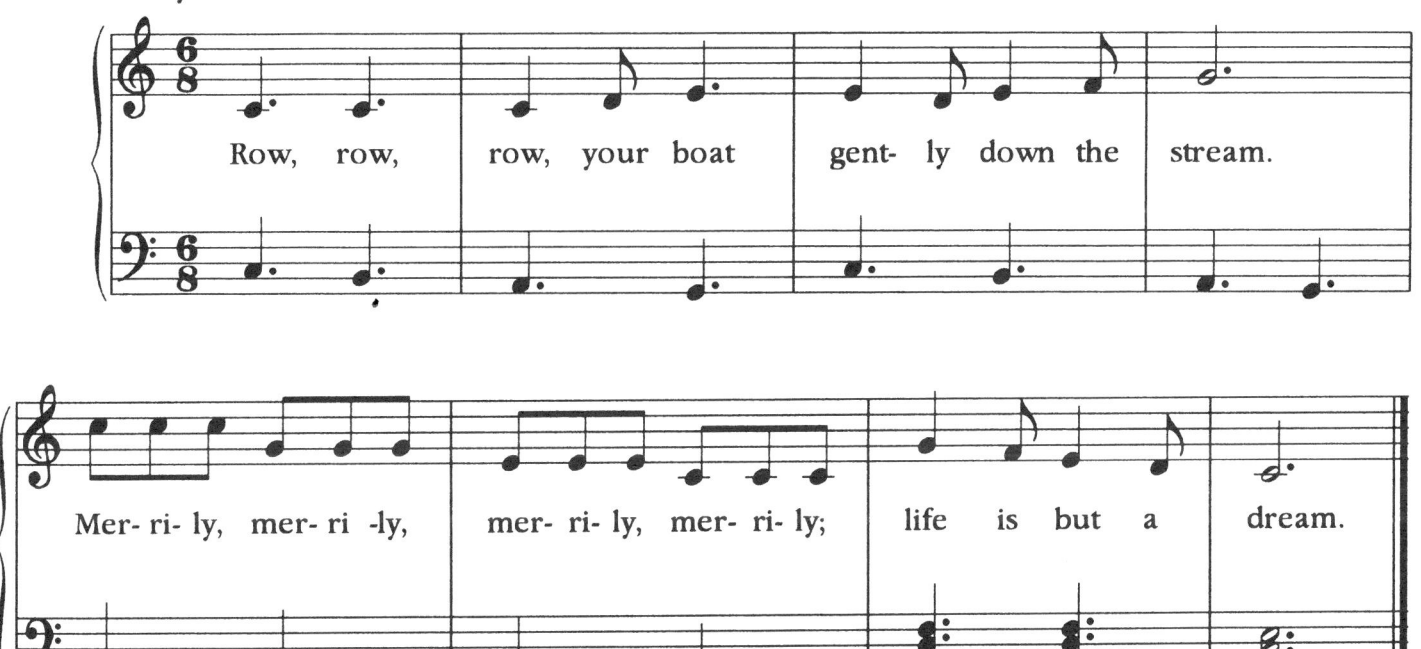

Lively

Row, row,   row, your boat   gent- ly down the   stream.

Mer- ri- ly, mer- ri -ly,   mer- ri- ly, mer- ri- ly;   life   is   but   a   dream.

Lavender's Blue

Joyfully

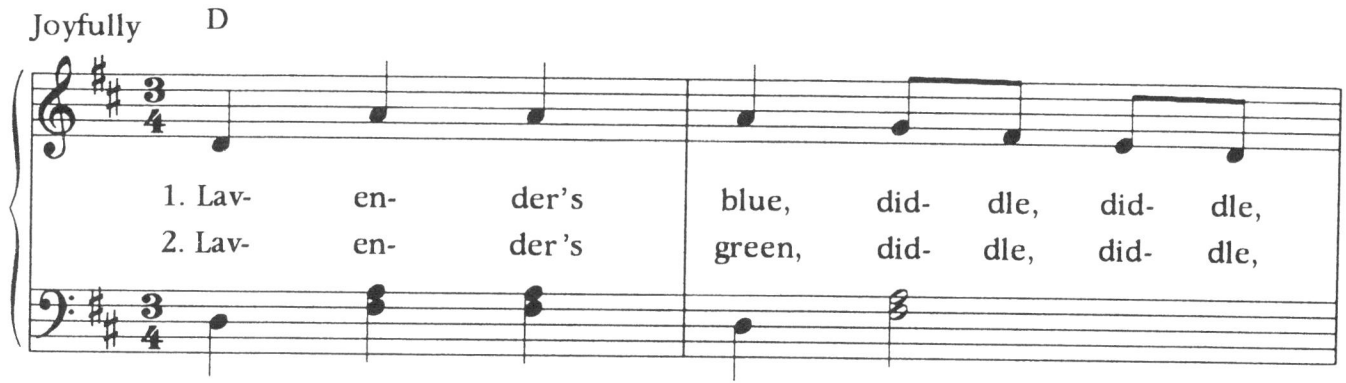

Shoo, Fly

Traditional

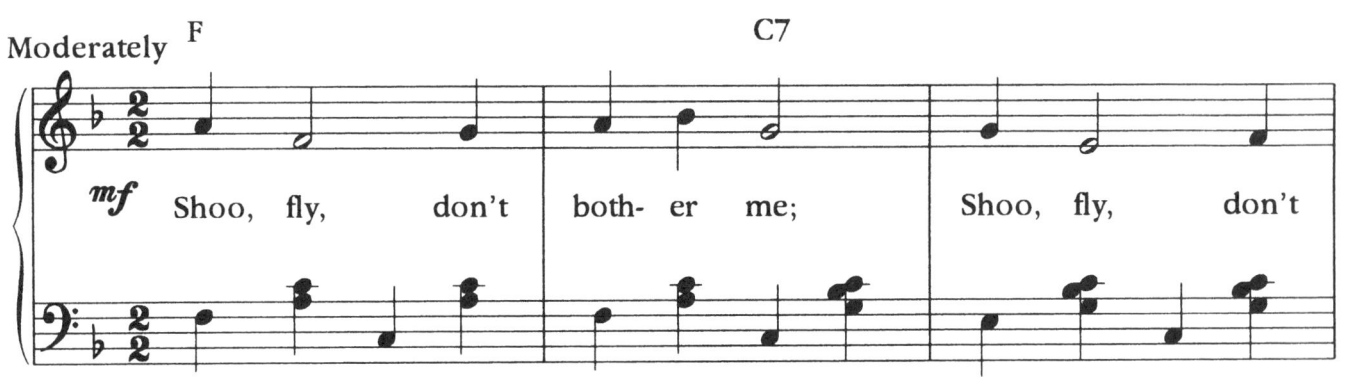

Shortnin' Bread

Traditional

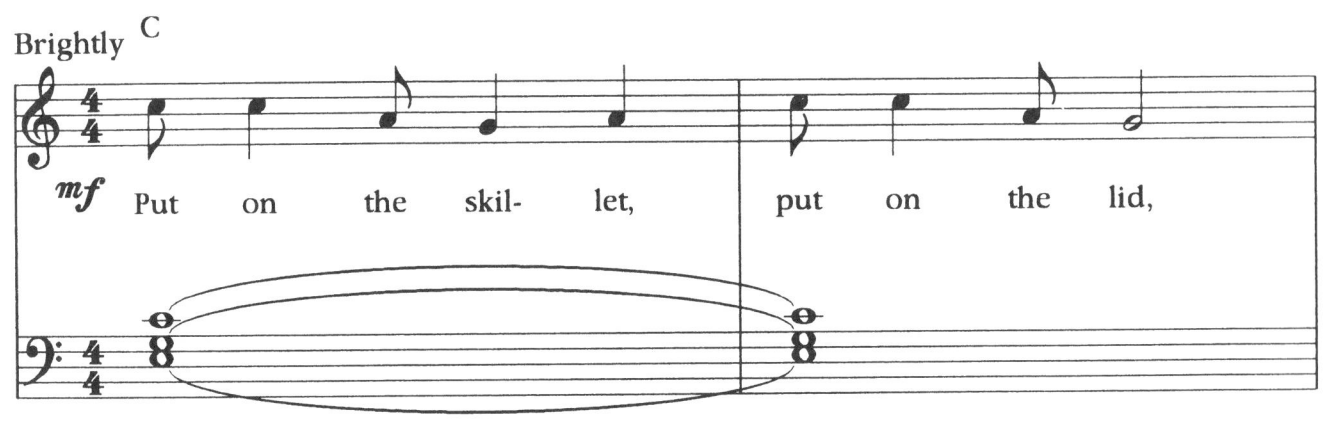

Brightly   C

mf Put on the skil- let, put on the lid,

G7   C

ma- ma's gon- na make a lit- tle short- nin' bread.

That ain't all she's gon- na do;——

G7   C

Ma- ma's gon- na make a lit- tle cof- fee, too.

Ma- ma's lit- tle ba- by loves short - nin', short - nin',

G7   C

ma- ma's lit- tle ba- by loves short- nin' bread.

Ma- ma's lit- tle- ba- by loves short- nin', short- nin',

G7   C

ma - ma's lit- tle ba- by loves short nin' - bread

Rock-A-Bye, Baby

Traditional

Slowly

Rock- a- bye,   ba-   by,   on the tree   top,

when the wind   blows   the   cra- dle will   rock:

When the bough   breaks   the   cra- dle will   fall,   and

down will come   bab-   by,   cra- dle and   all.

Sing A Song Of Sixpence

Mother Goose

2. The king was in his counting house, counting out his

money;

The queen was in the parlor, eating bread and honey.

The maid was in the garden, hanging out the clothes;

Along came a blackbird and snipped off her nose.

Mary Had A Little Lamb

Mother Goose

3. Followed her to school one day, school one day,
School one day,
Followed her to school one day, which was against
The rules.

4. Made the children laugh and play, laugh and play,
Laugh and play,
Made the children laugh and play to see a lamb at
School.

A Tisket, A Tasket

Traditional

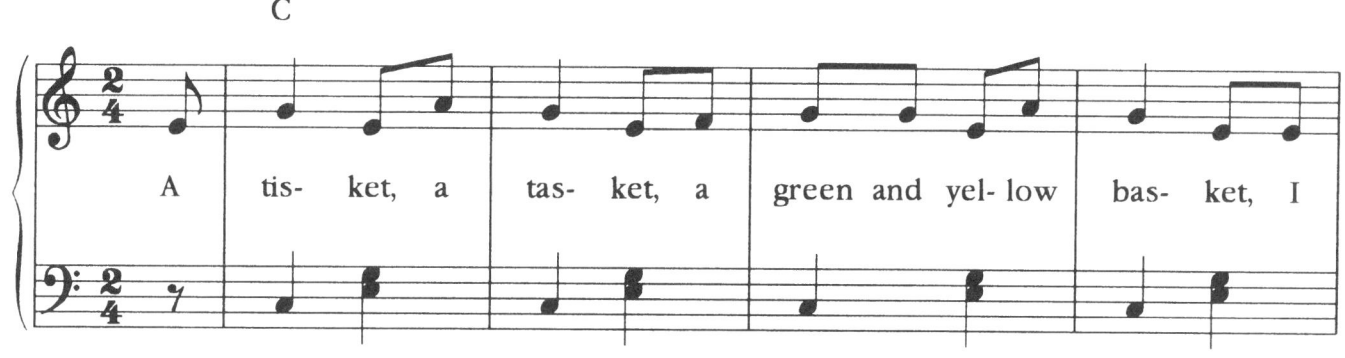

Cradle Song (Brahms's Lullaby)

Brahms

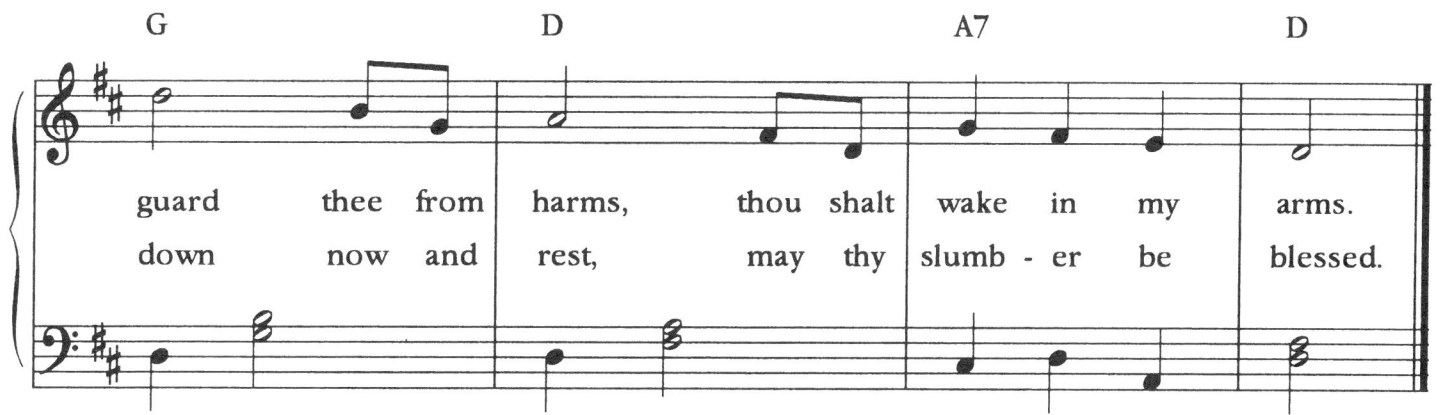

G D A7 D
guard thee from harms, thou shalt wake in my arms.
down now and rest, may thy slumb - er be blessed.

The Alphabet Song

Mother Goose

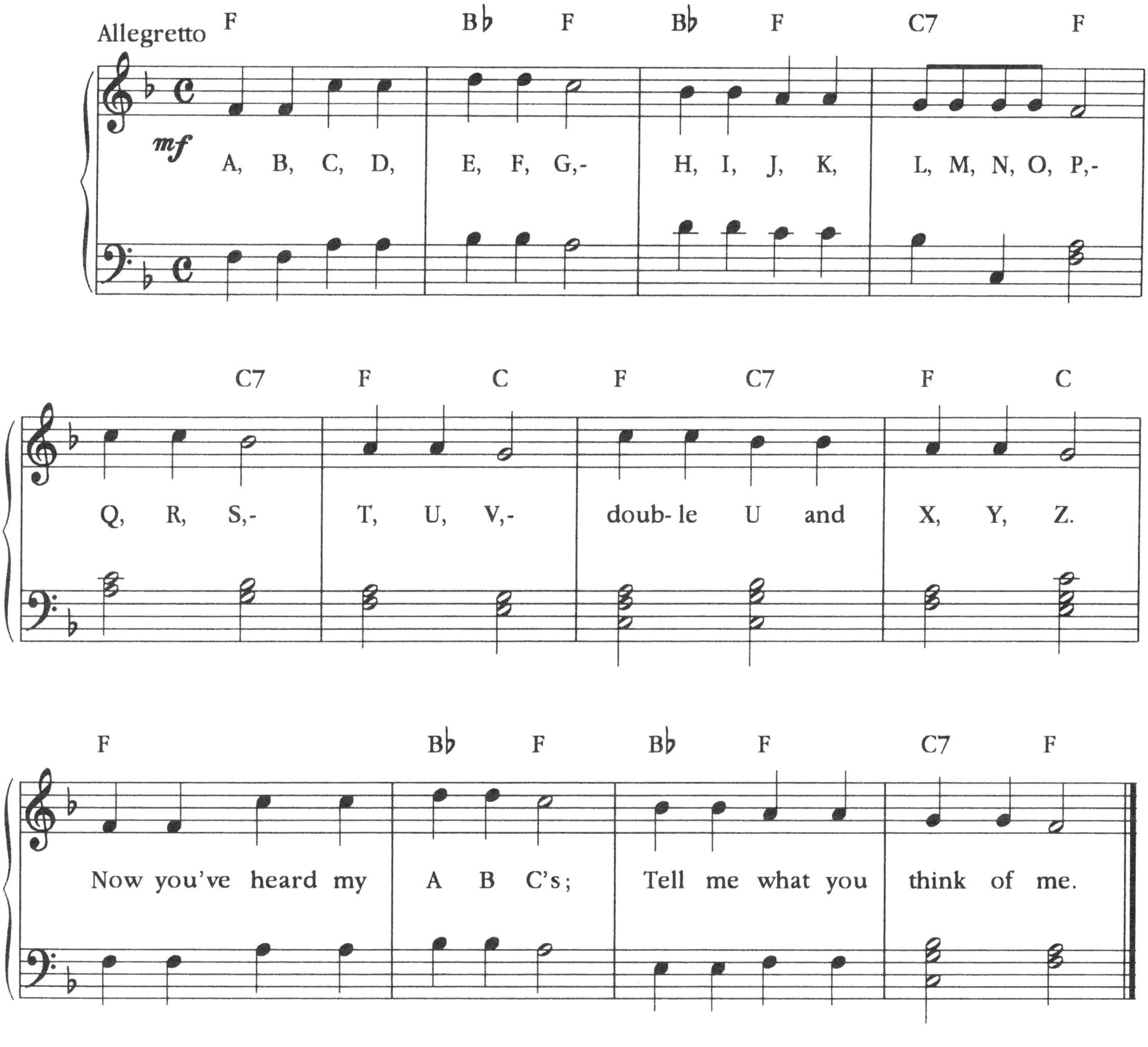

Allegretto
mf
F Bb F Bb F C7 F
A, B, C, D, E, F, G,- H, I, J, K, L, M, N, O, P,-
C7 F C F C7 F C
Q, R, S,- T, U, V,- doub- le U and X, Y, Z.
F Bb F Bb F C7 F
Now you've heard my A B C's; Tell me what you think of me.

The Spider And The Fly

Traditional

Moderately

F

1. Will you walk in- to my par- lour?" said the
2. way in- to my par- lour ——— is

B♭   C7

spi- der to the fly; " 'Tis the pret- tiest lit- tle
up a wind- ing stair, and ——— I have man- y

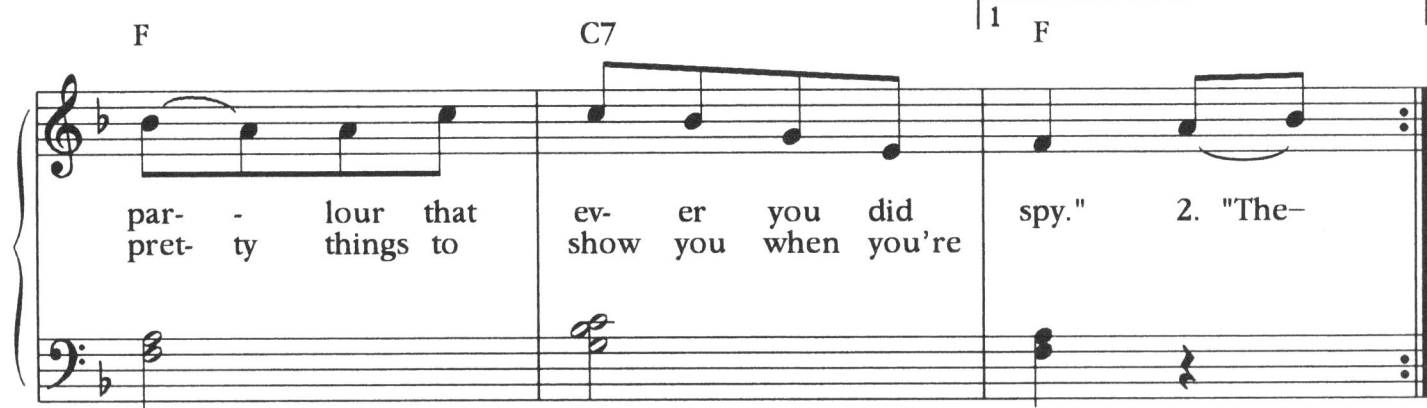

F   C7   1. F

par - lour that ev- er you did spy." 2. "The—
pret- ty things to show you when you're

2. F

there." "Oh, no, no!" said the lit- tle fly, "To

ask me is in vain. For who goes up your

wind- ing stair shall ne're come down a- gain."

Skip To My Lou

Traditional

2. Little red wagon painted blue,
   Little red wagon painted blue,
   Little red wagon painted blue,
   Skip to my Lou, my darling.

3. Flies in the buttermilk, shoo fly shoo,
   Flies in the buttermilk, shoo fly shoo,
   Flies in the buttermilk, shoo fly shoo,
   Skip to my lou, my darling.

4. Lost my partner, what'll I do,
   Lost my partner, what'll I do,
   Lost my partner, what'll I do,
   Skip to my Lou, my darling.

5. I'll get another one, prettier than you,
   I'll get another one, prettier than you,
   I'll get another one, prettier than you,
   Skip to my Lou, my darling.

This Old Man

Traditional

2. This old man, he played two;

   He played knick-knack on my shoe.

   Chorus;

3. This old man, he played three,

   He played knick-knack on my knee.

   Chorus;

4. This old man, he played four,

   He played knick-knack on my door.

   Chorus;

5. This old man, he played five,

   He played knick-knack on my hive.

   Chorus;

6. This old man, he played six,

   He played knick-knack on my sticks.

   Chorus;

7. This old man, he played seven,

   He played knick-knack up to heaven.

   Chorus;

8. This old man, he played eight,

   He played knick-knack at the gate.

   Chorus;

9. This old man, he played nine,

   He played knick-knack on my line.

   Chorus;

10. This old man, he played ten,

    He played knick-knack over again.

    Chorus;

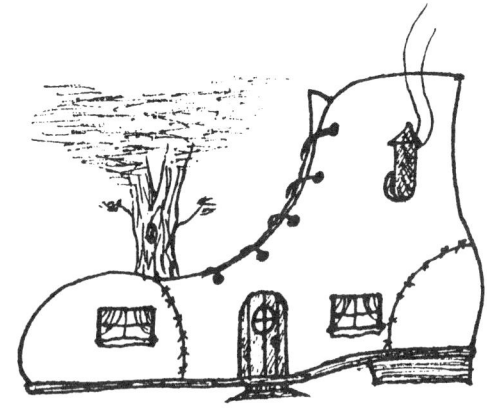

There Was An Old Woman

Mother Goose

Moderately

| Gm | Cm | Gm | D7 | Gm |

mp

There was an old wo-man who lived — in a shoe, she

| Eb | Bb | F7 | Bb |

had so man- y chil- dren she did- n't know what to do. She

| Bb 7 | Eb | Bb | Cm7 | D |

gave them some broth with out an- y bread, and

| Gm | Cm | Gm | Eb7 | (D+) | Gm | D7 | Gm |

whipped them all sound- ly, and sent - them to bed.

Ride A Cock-Horse To Banbury Cross

Three Little Kittens

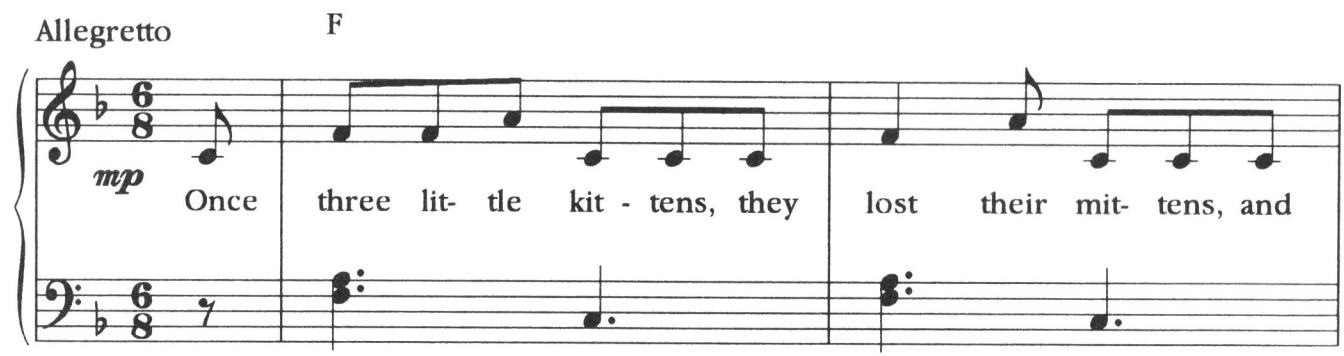

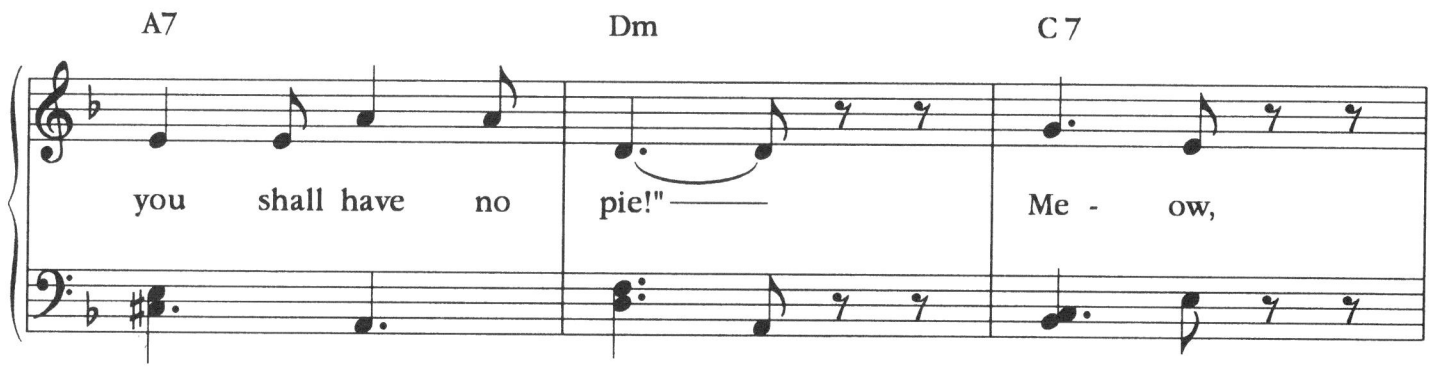

you shall have no pie!"——— Me - ow,

Me - ow, Me - ow, Me - ow,

Me - ow, Me - ow, Meow.———

2. The three little kittens they found their mittens

and they began to cry: "Oh Mommy dear,

See here, see here our mittens we have found."

"What Found your mittens you darling kittens,

Then you shall have some pie."

Chorus:

3. The three little kittens, put on their mittens,

And soon ate up the pie. "Oh Mommy dear,

We greatly fear our mittens we have soiled."

"What! Soiled your mittens? You naughty kittens."

Then they began to sigh.

Three Little Pigs

Traditional

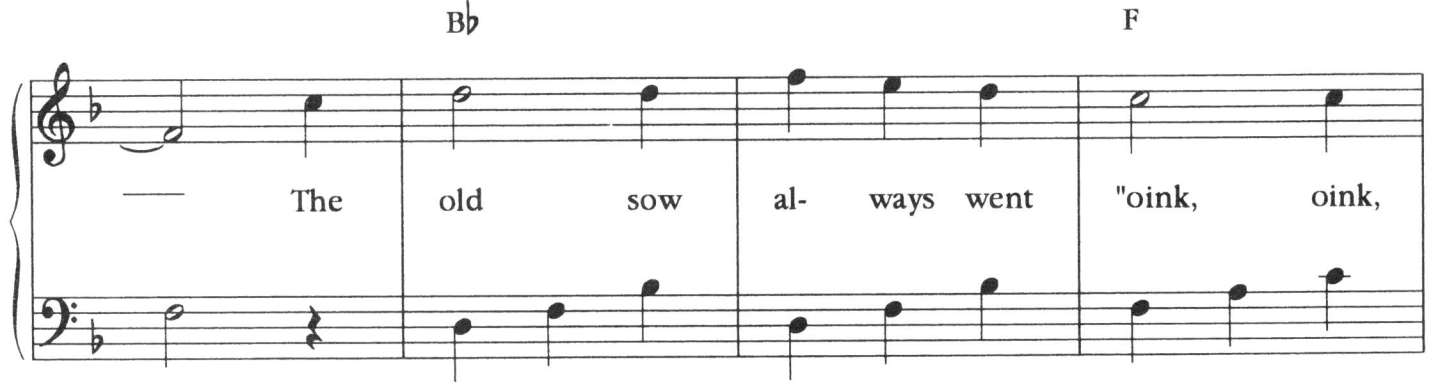

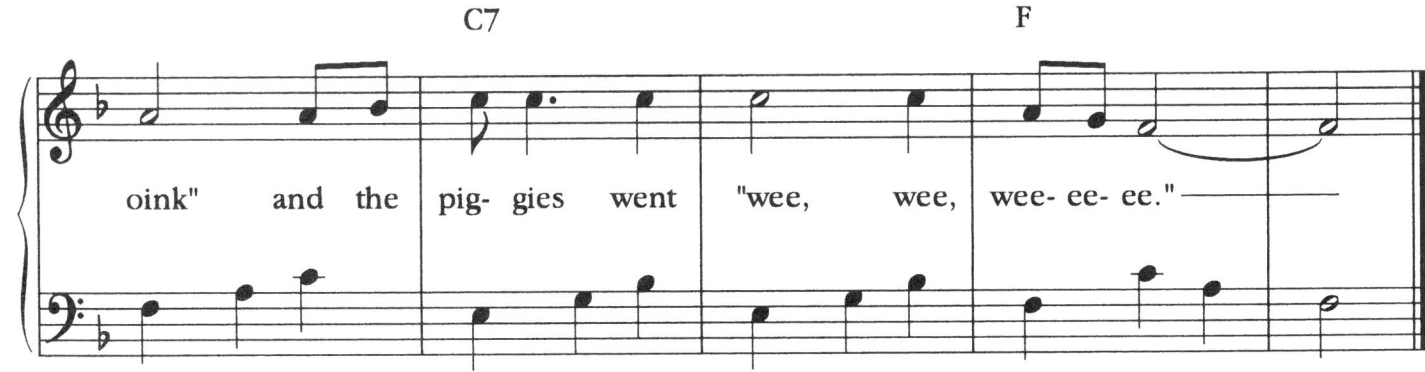

2. Now one day, one of the three little pigs,
   To the other two piggies said he,
   "Why don't we always go "oink, oink, oink?"
   It's so childish to go wee, wee-ee-ee."

3. These three little piggies grew skinny and lean,
   Skinny they well should be;
   For they always would try to go "oink, oink, oink,"
   And they wouldn't go "wee, wee, wee-ee-ee."

4. Now these three piggies then up and they died,
   What a lesson that should be:
   Don't ever try to go "oink, oink, oink,"
   When you ought to go "wee, wee, wee-ee-ee."

Go In And Out
The Window

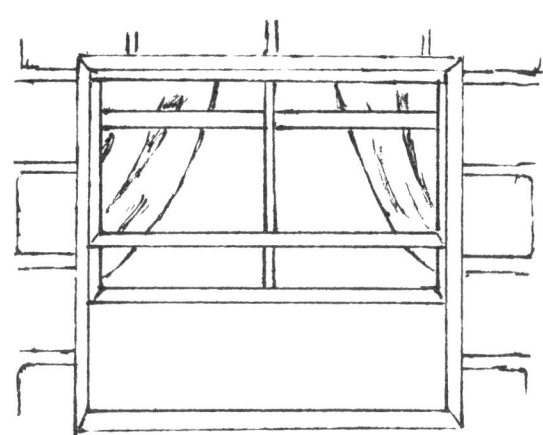

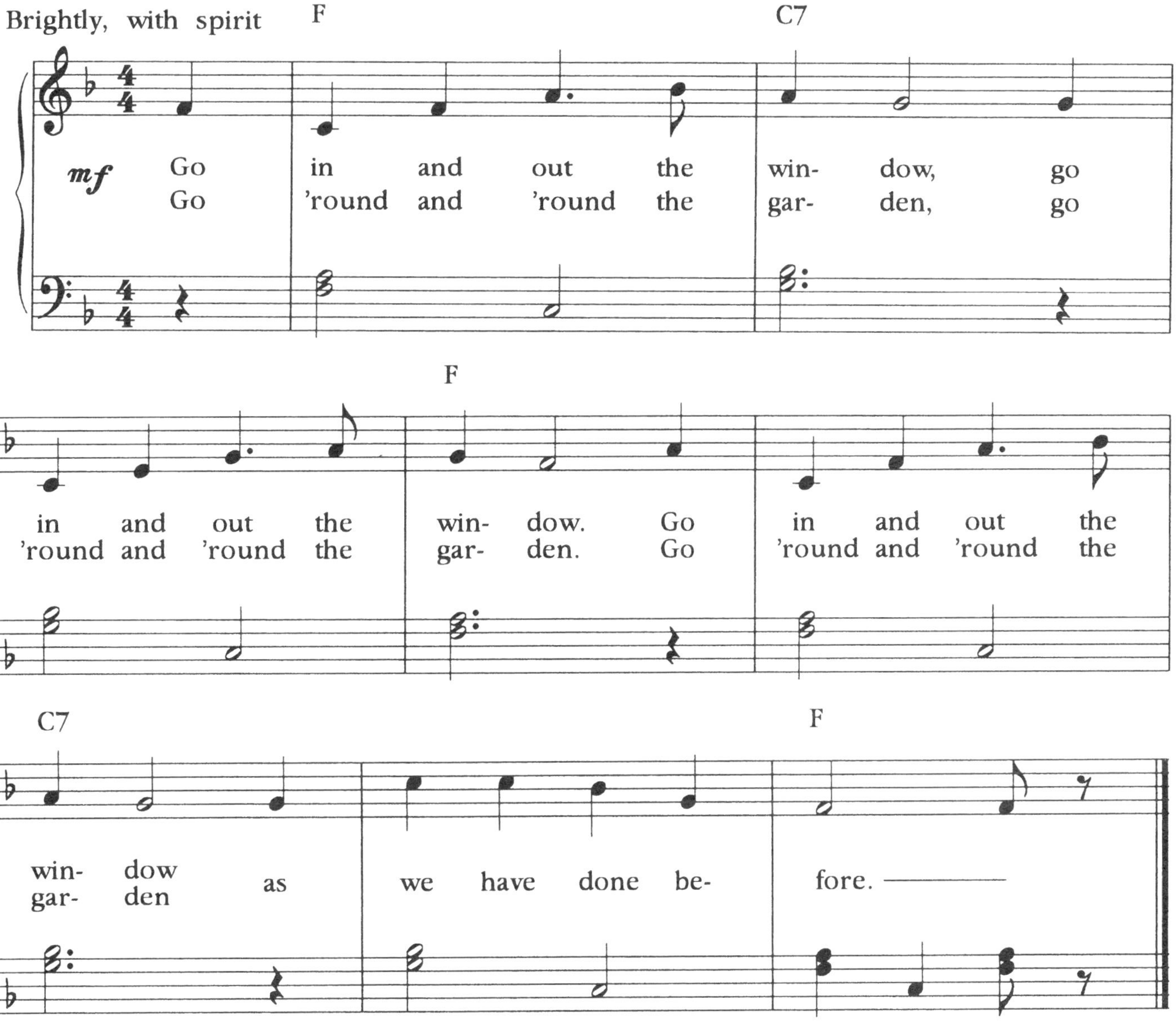

Brightly, with spirit

F

mf Go in and out the win- dow, go
Go 'round and out 'round the gar- den, go

C7

F

in and out the win- dow. Go
'round and 'round the gar- den. Go

in and out the
'round and 'round the

C7

win- dow as we have done be- fore. ———
gar- den

F

Twinkle, Twinkle, Little Star

Traditional

Where Is Thumbkin?

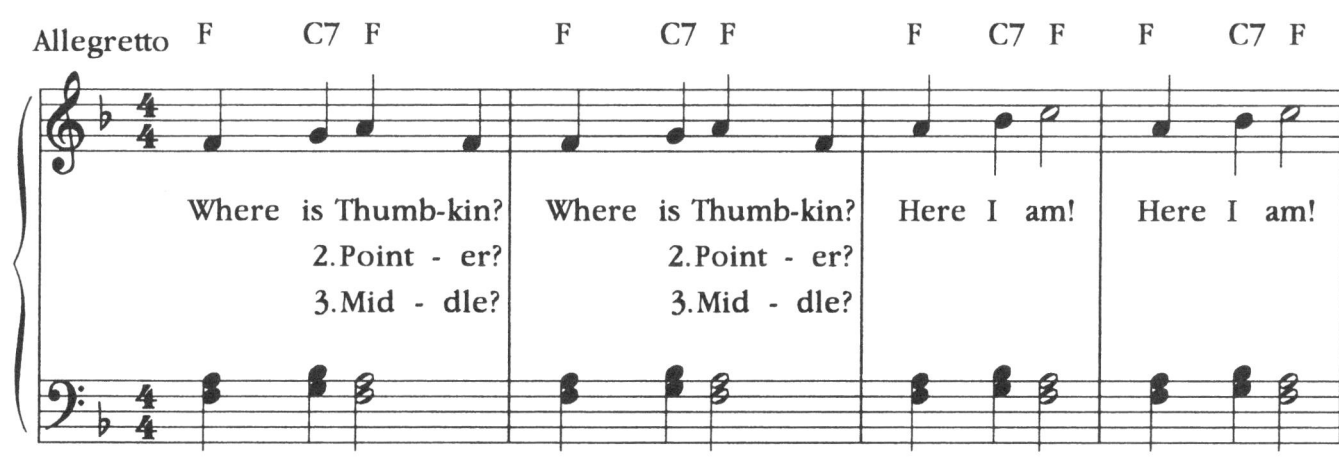

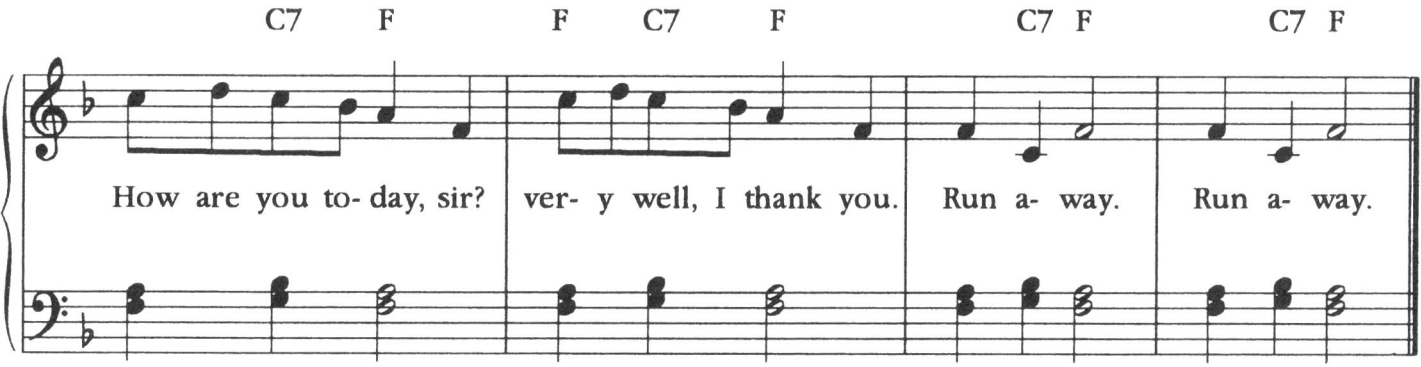

I've Been Working On The Railroad

Folk Song

Music Dictionary

Accompany (comp) - *To play background music that compliments or enhances a melody.*

Anticipation - *A note played a little before the beat.*

Accent > - *Play with emphasis.*

Chord - *Two or more notes played at the same time.*

Chord Symbols - *The letter above the staff that indicates the chord to play.*

Crescendo < - *Gradually louder.*

Diminuendo > - *Gradually softer.*

Dynamic Markings - *p - soft   mf - moderately loud   f - loud*

Fade Out - *The song does not have a definite ending, so it ends by getting softer until there is no more sound.*

Flat ♭ - *Play the next note lower in pitch.*

Harmony - *Playing more than one note at a time.*

Incomplete Measures - *The first and last measures are incomplete by themselves, but form a complete measure together.*

Intervals

    Melodic Interval - *The distance between two notes played consecutively.*

    Harmonic Interval - *The distance between two notes played together.*

Improvisation - *The art of creating music on the spot.*

Lead Sheet - *A treble staff with only the melody, words, and chords written. You create the rest of the arrangement.*

Legato - *Play smoothly with no breaks between the notes.*

Melody - *A series of notes played in succession form a melody. Most songs are recognized by the melody.*

Metronome - *A device that clicks the beat at a tempo you select.*

Natural ♮ - *Cancels out a sharp or a flat.*

Phrase - *A musical sentence.*

Rhythm - *Duration of notes.*

Sharp ♯ - *Play the next key higher in pitch.*

Staccato · - *Play short and detached.*

Staff ≡ - *A set of five horizontal lines on which music notes are written.*

Swing - *Play the first of two eighth notes longer and the second of two eighth notes shorter.*

Tempo - *Describes speed, character, and/or style of a piece.*

Transpose - *Changing the notes from one position to another.*

Walking Bass - *A bass line used in swing. The rhythm is usually all quarter notes and sounds like the bass is walking, hence it's name.*

1st & 2nd Endings - *Play 1st ending only, then repeat and play the 2nd ending only.*

8va - *Play one octave (8 notes) higher than written.*

* For a more complete Music Dictionary, Encyclopedia of Music Knowledge by Dr. William F. Lee, Santorella Publications is recommended.

TEACHER'S AID PRODUCTS

Keyboard Kids "Flash Cards"
All books $10.95
Volume 1 • TS224
Volume 2 • TS225
Volume 3 • TS226

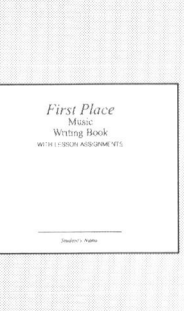

Each volume is contained in an 80 page hard bound book with perforated card stock which is easily removed. Rather than fumbling with loose cards and a rubber band...keep them all neatly wrapped up in you very own hard cover edition. These easy tear-out cards contain music symbols introduced in a logical manner but may be rearranged in any desired rotation. A perfect tool for classroom study or one on one with Mom & Dad.

Dictionary of Musical Terms
TS220 • $7.95
Encyclopedia of Music Knowledge
TS221 • $10.95

Packed with over 2,500 concisely defined music terms and theory reference charts. The dictionary serves as a fantastic quick guide glossary of terms and the Encyclopedia covers it all: Scales, modes, intervals, transposition, ranges, conducting patterns and a chronological timeline of music history. An absolute must for any student of music.

Music Writing Paper
HM001 • $5.95   64 pages, 12 stave spiral with perforation.
HM002 • $4.95   64 pages, 10 stave stitch with perforation.
HM004 • $4.95
6 stave with practice lesson record and dictionary.

Basic Guitar Writing Book
OGB45 • $4.95   Tab & Standard staves with chord boxes.

Basic Bass Guitar Writing Book
OGB46 • $4.95   64 perforated pages with tab and chord boxes.

Keyboard Kids "Wide Line" Manuscript Book
TS205 • $3.95   4 stave, 64 perforated pages.

Keyboard Kids Quiet 88 Reversible Keyboard
TS206 • $4.95

That's right! All 88 keys. One side this "actual size" piano keyboard is meant for table-top practice, hence the name: "Quiet 88". The opposite side sets right behind the keys on your baby grand. A mirror image of the keyboard indicating octaves, scales, notes and enharmonics. From top to bottom & front to back, it's got it all!

SANTORELLA PUBLICATIONS, LTD.
13 Pleasant Avenue   **Danvers, MA 01923**   **www.santorellapublications.com**